Fig. 3
William Clayton
From *Iron Workers, Tredegar, Wales*
1865

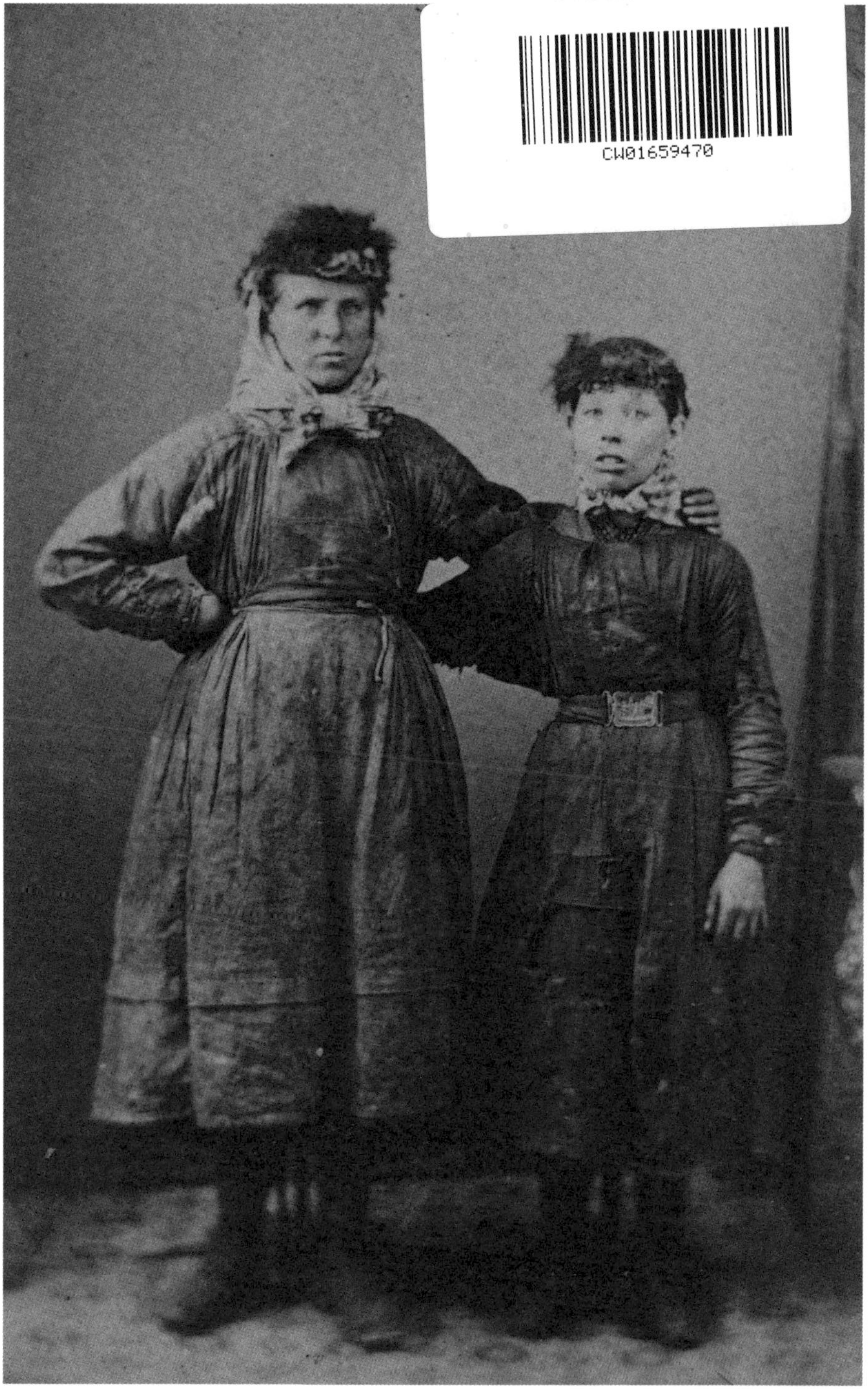

The photographs were taken in response to a debate surrounding the role of women in industry. One letter writer in the *Merthyr Telegraph*, 1865, pointed out that 'working men complain that their wives are of very little use to them as help-meets. They can't make their children's clothes and they can't cook...' Another expressed concern over the impact of physical work on reproductive health: 'The employment of the physically weak in labours demanding great physical exertion, tends to lessen the capacity of throwing off diseases, and gradually dwarfs the physical frame... when these females become the mothers of the succeeding generation, we find the offspring debilitated by the weakness of the parent.'

Their attempts to add a femininity to their appearance is notable in its marked contrast to the harsh labour they are performing.

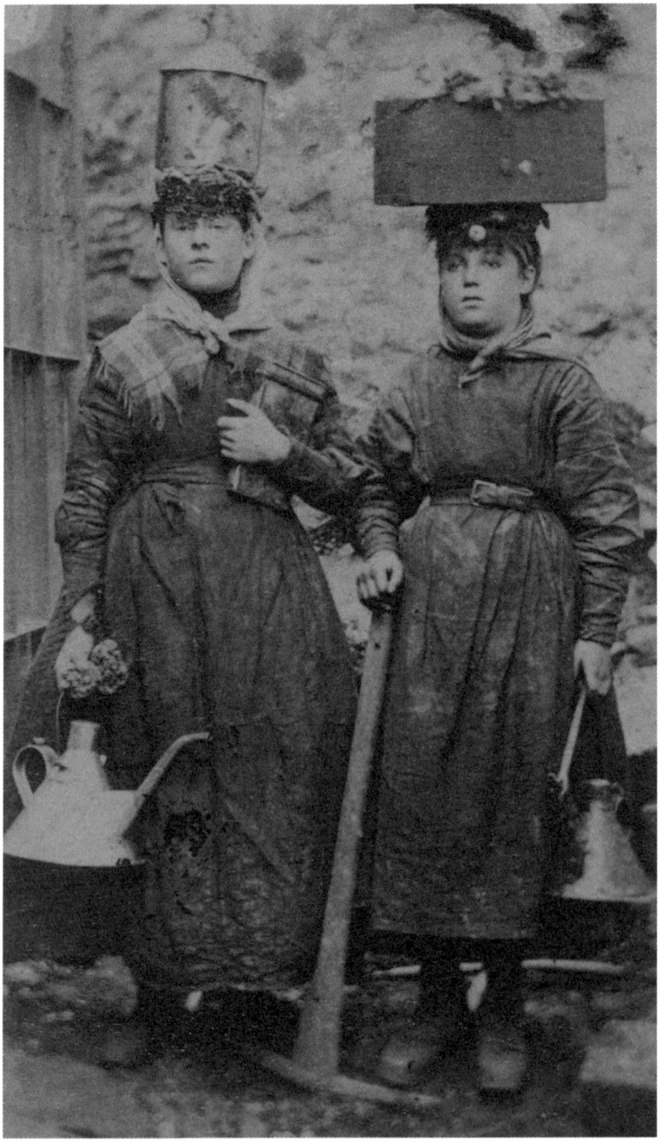

'The bonnet or hat, for it is difficult to discern to which of these classes this head-dress belongs, is bedecked with beads, brooches and feathers, the latter addition in a way imitating the Prince of Wales plume. In this dress, with faces black with dust and smoke, it is difficult, when elevated 50 or 100 yards, to discern the sex to which these objects belong; and a gentleman, who evidently had never witnessed such a sight before, on visiting the town of Tredegar recently, expressed his astonishment at making mountains on mountains and inquired what animals those were he saw moving about on the top? In the tempest and the storm, in rain and in snow, in the sun and heat, exposed to all weathers, women and girls are employed on the tips in South Wales.' — *Bristol Mercury*, 29 April 1865

Fig. 4
William Clayton
From *Iron Workers, Tredegar, Wales*
1865

Fig. 5
William Clayton
From *Iron Workers, Tredegar, Wales*
1865

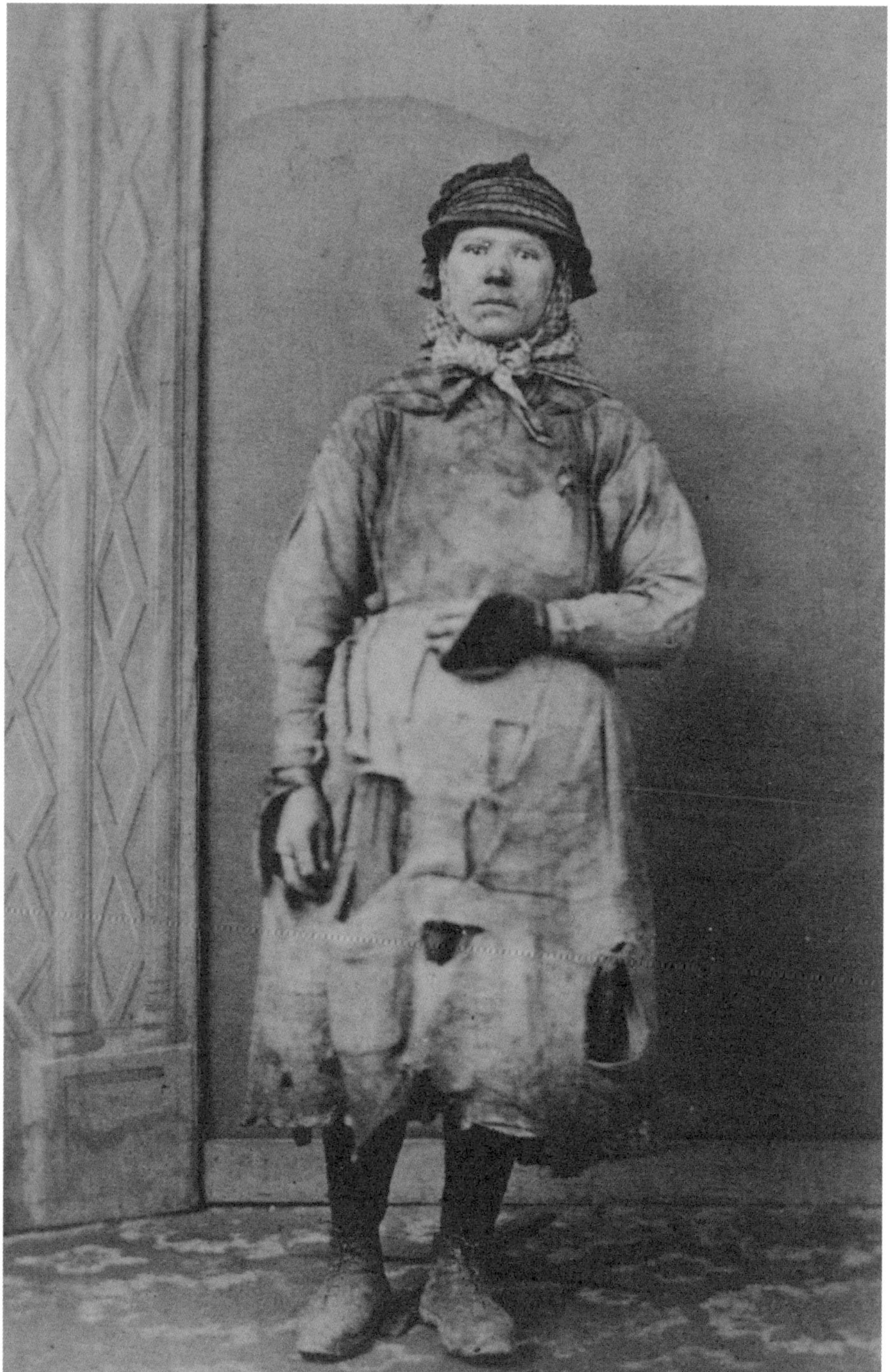

Fig. 6
John Martin
The Destruction of Sodom and Gomorrah
1852

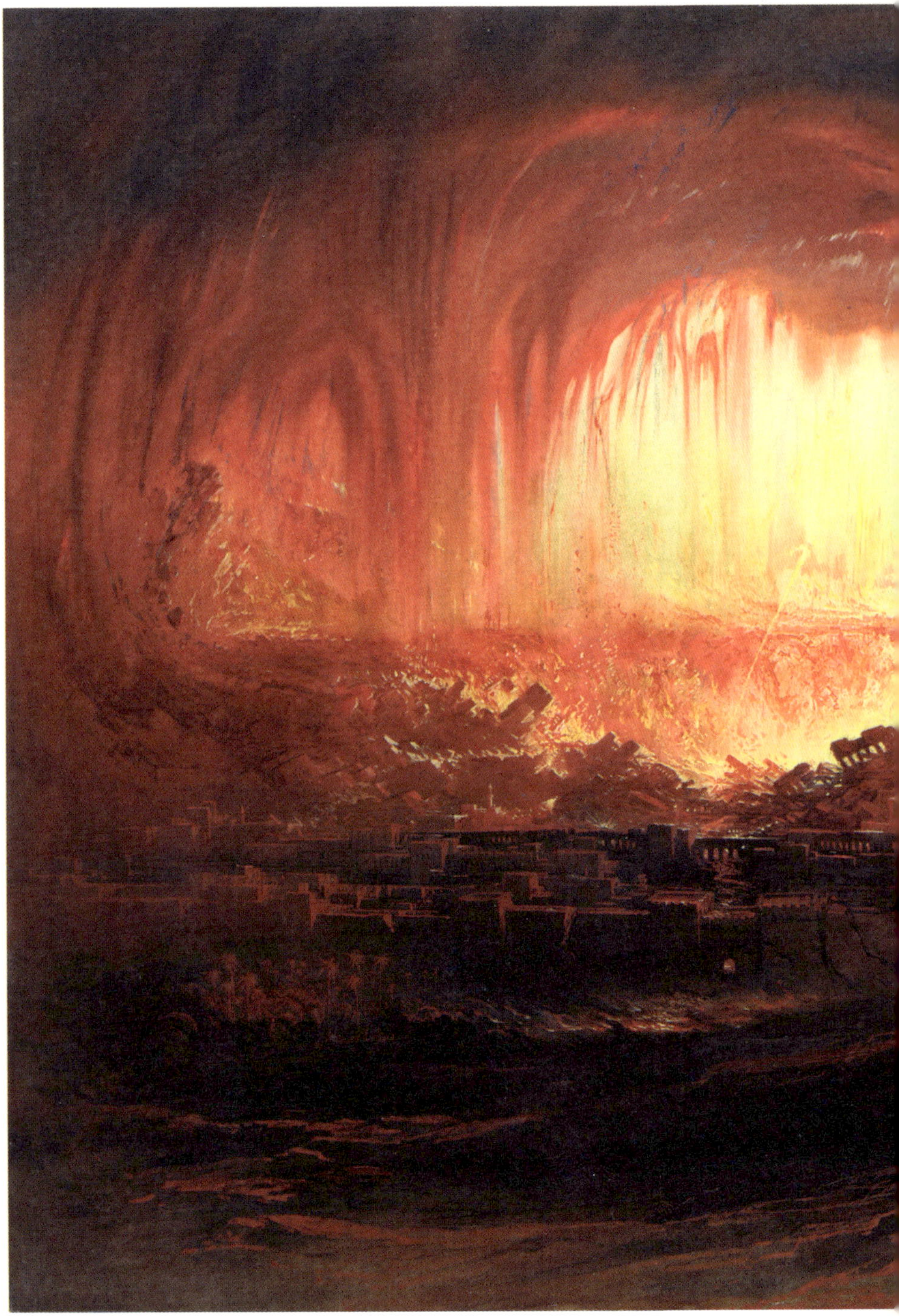

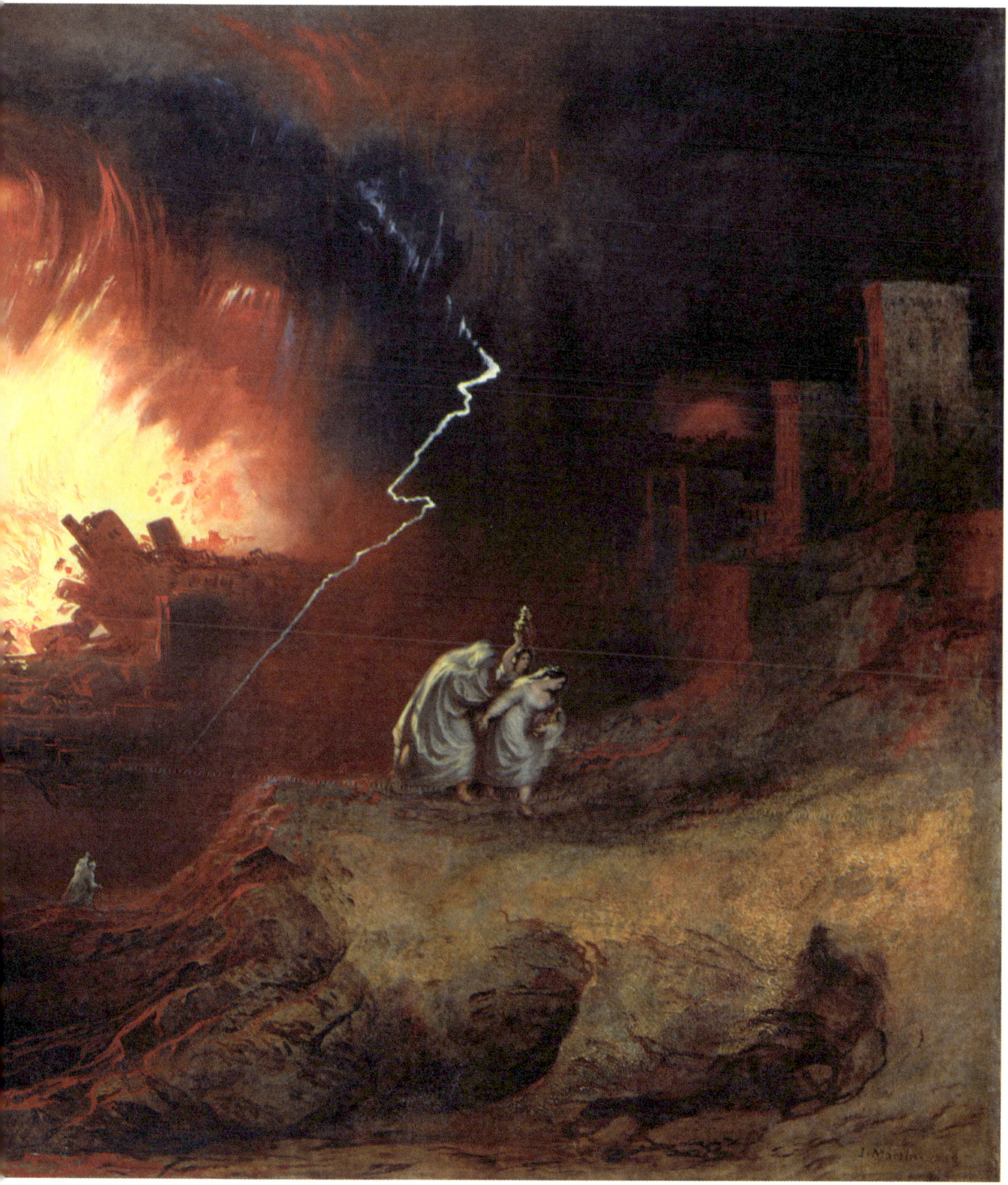

Thirteen years earlier, John Martin was also depicting the anxieties of the age in his masterpiece *The Destruction of Sodom and Gomorrah*, a painting as much about the mid-Victorian period as the distant ancient world it depicts. It serves as a warning about the potential implosion of society, as the city destroys itself under the weight of its sin and disease – two problems that, for many Victorians, were inextricably linked. The industrial boom of the early 1800s had caused an unprecedented exodus of the rural poor to urban centres; by 1851, for the first time in human history, more people in the nation were living in cities than in the countryside. The population of London was 2.6 million and this rapid urbanisation caused huge infrastructural problems. Water, which had previously been drawn from wells and streams, was now a bringer of death. Polluted by factory waste-products and sewage, the river Irwell in Salford went purple and foamed with noxious gases.

Two years before *The Destruction of Sodom and Gomorrah* was completed thousands had died in the 1848–49 London cholera epidemic – a man-made near-apocalypse. Martin would have been well aware of this: he was obsessed with the sewage problem faced by the largest city in the world and for over 20 years had been lecturing, publishing plans and lobbying parliament on the subject. In 1845 he formed the joint-stock Metropolitan Sewage and Manure Company, tasked with creating a system that would remove the waste to the rapidly industrialising farmland of the South East. As well as being needed to boost production and cope with the population increase, it was also envisaged that the public works would put the unemployed to better use than the workhouse: a punitive parody of the factory. This only served to enhance his visionary credentials, but his ambitious schemes invited much public ridicule, with *Punch* magazine commenting, in 1843, that he was 'positively pathetic about having devoted a long and arduous life to the sewers and cesspools of his native city, 14 long years had he laboured to enlarge the subterranean ways and water courses of the modern Babylon'. Martin was vindicated shortly after his death with the construction of a large-scale sewage system in London, which bore a resemblance to his own plan and its ambitions.

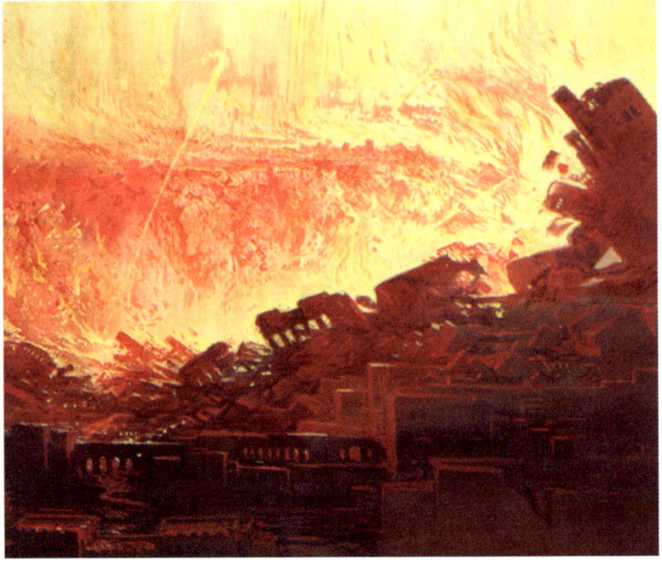

Fig. 7
John Martin
The Destruction of Sodom and Gomorrah (detail)
1852

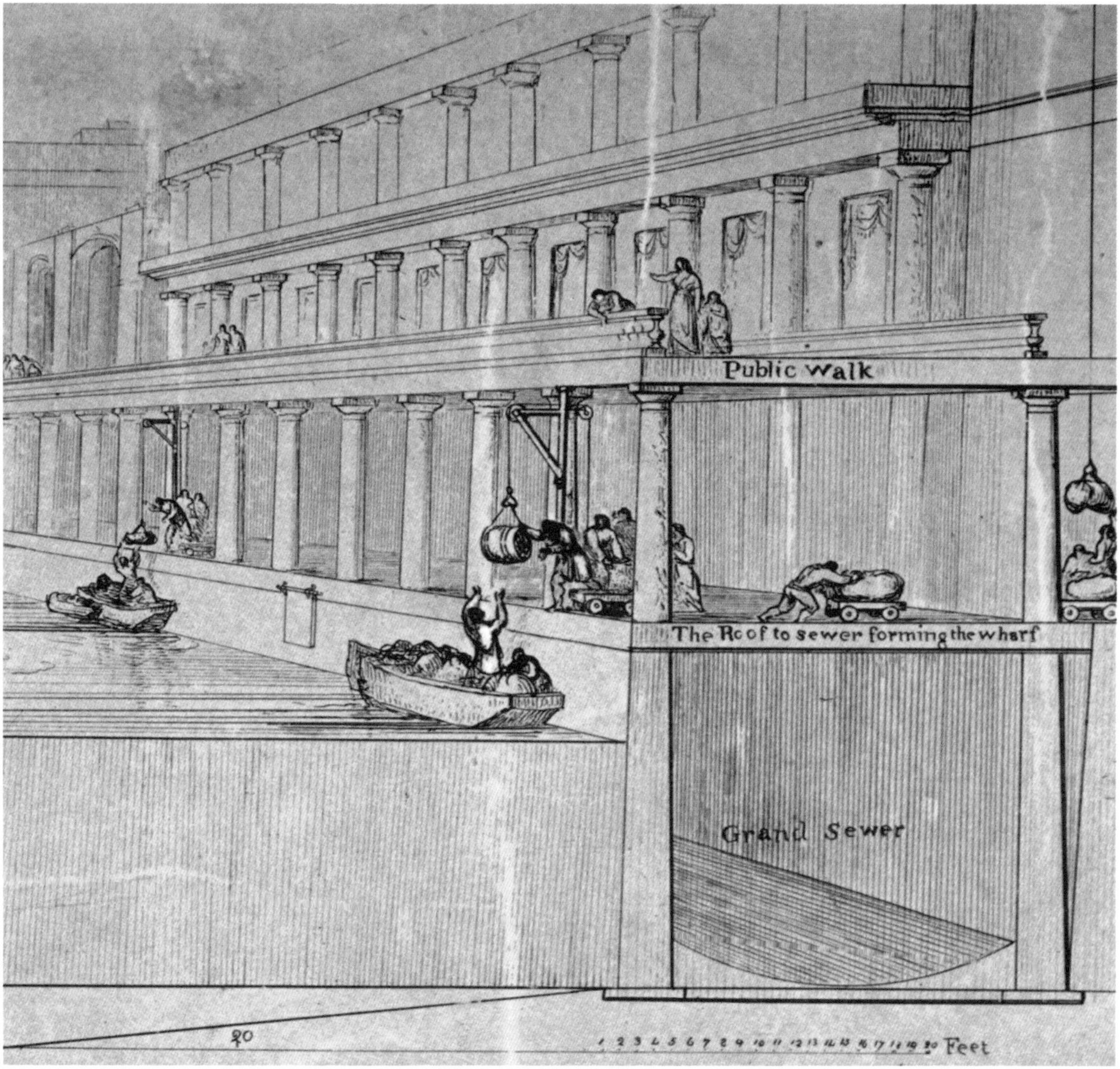

Fig. 8
John Martin
Plan for Preventing the Pollution of the Water of the Thames
1834

'Plan for preventing the pollution of the water of the Thames and preserving the sewage for agricultural purposes, by means of Grand Sewers running parallel with each bank, into which all the minor drains should fall. Wharfs should be so constructed as to form the roof of the sewer; with a grand public walk forming a roof to the wharf, the three combined objects would cost little more than either of the three separate; whilst the utility, grandeur and proportionate value of the property would be greatly increased.'
— John Martin, 2 June 1834

Fig. 9
G. Greatbach
The Black Country,
Near Bilston
1869

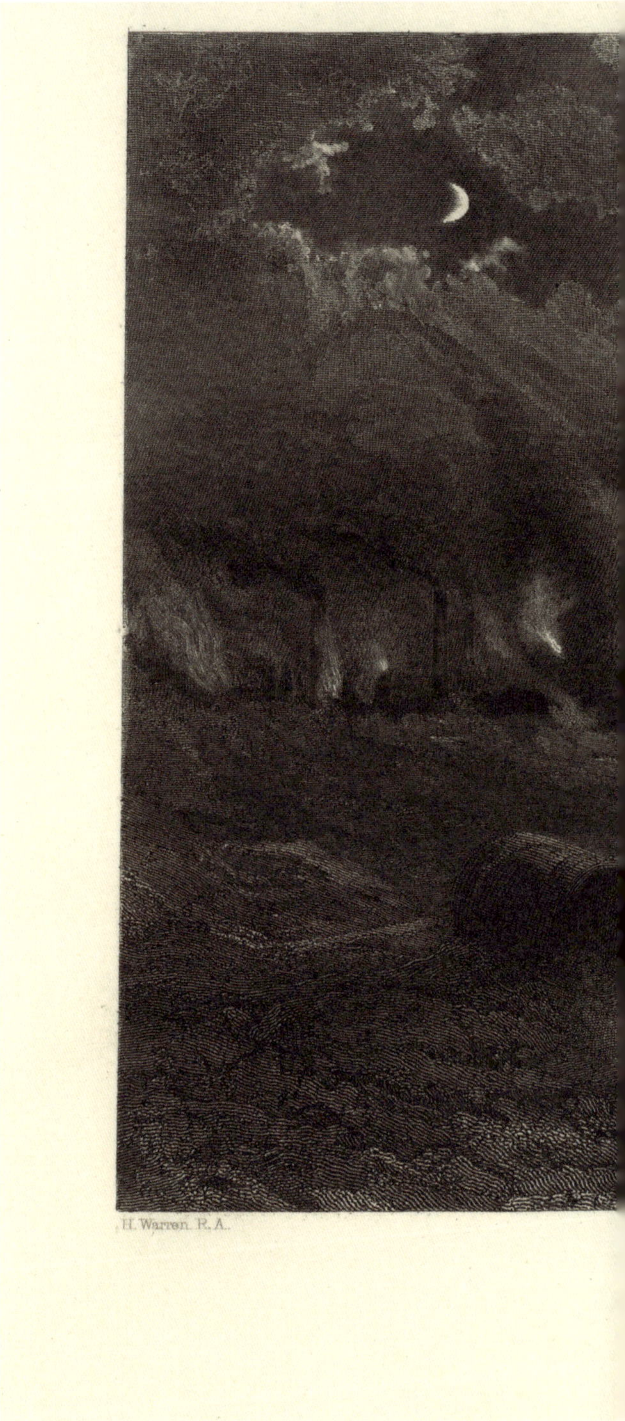

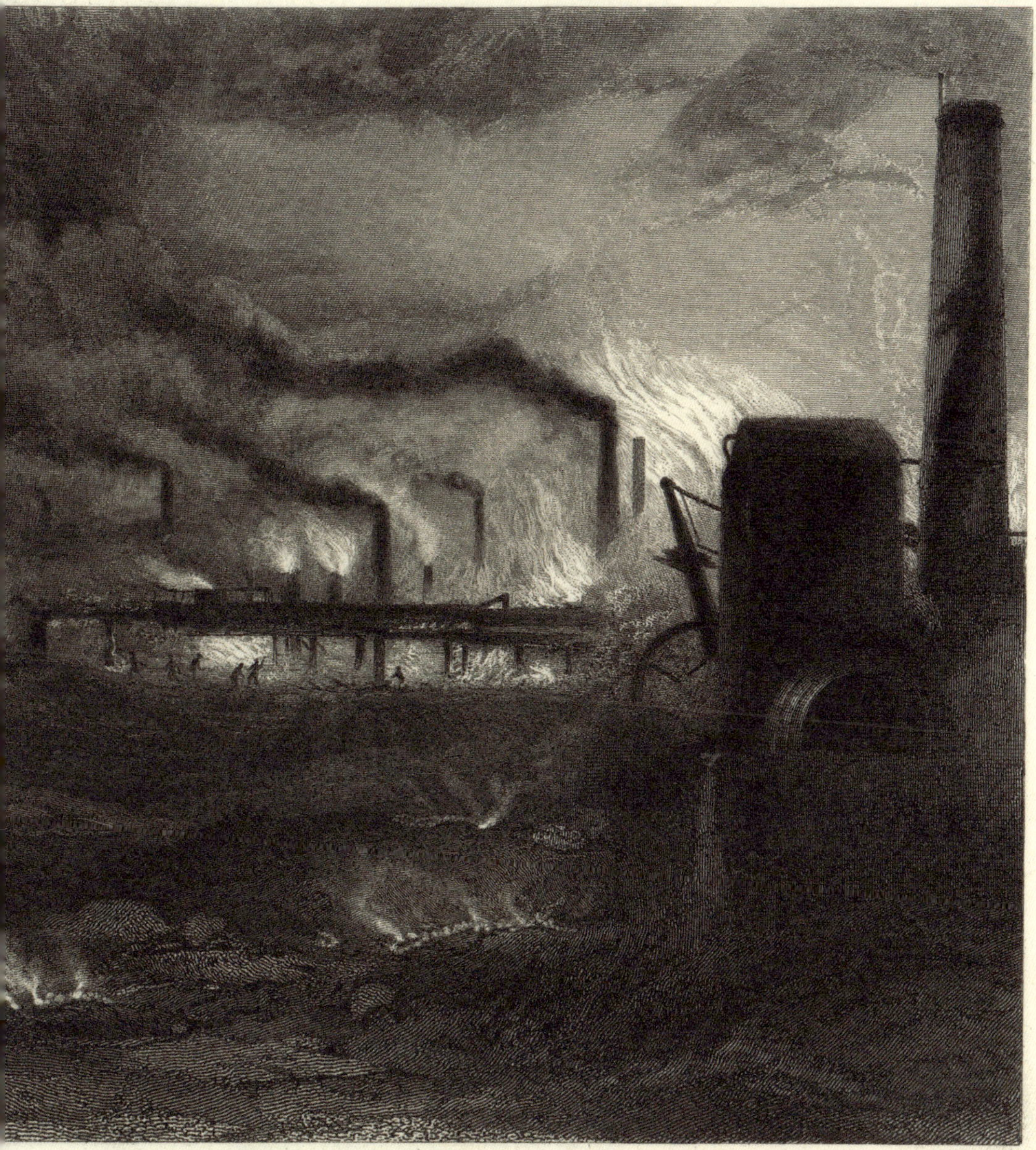

G. Greatbach.

HE BLACK COUNTRY.

(NEAR BILSTON)

A fellow engineer also saw industrial chaos in similarly epic terms:

'The Black Country is anything but picturesque. The earth seems to have been turned inside out. Its entrails are strewn about; nearly the entire surface of the ground is covered with cinder heaps and mounds of scoriae. The coal, which has been drawn from below ground, is blazing on the surface. The district is crowded with iron furnaces, puddling furnaces and coal pit engine furnaces. By day and by night the country is glowing with fire, and the smoke of the ironworks hovers over it. Workmen covered with smut, and with fierce white eyes, are seen moving about amongst the glowing iron and dull thud of forge-hammers.

Amidst these flaming, smoky, clanging works, I beheld the remains of what had once been happy farmhouses, now ruined and deserted. The ground underneath them had sunk by the working out of the coal, and they were falling to pieces. They had in former times been surrounded by clumps of trees but only skeletons of them remained, dilapidated, black and lifeless. The grass had been parched and killed by the vapours of sulphurous acid thrown out by the chimneys; and every herbaceous object was a ghastly grey – the emblem of vegetable death in its saddest aspect. Vulcan had driven out Ceres.' — James Nasmyth, Engineer, *An Autobiography*, 1883

Fig. 10
G. F. Bragg
Treforest
Tin Works,
Glamorganshire
c. 1840

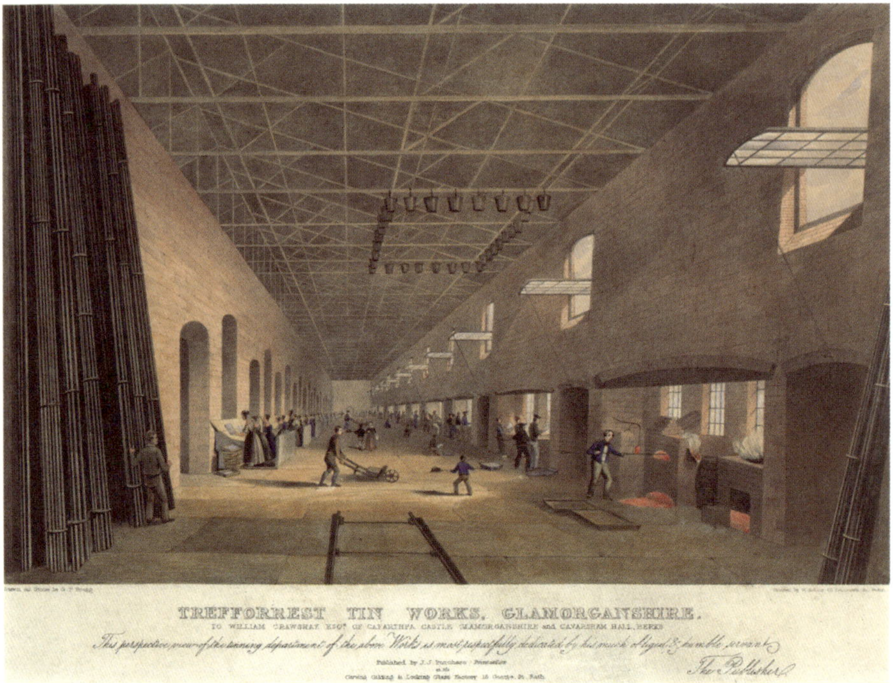

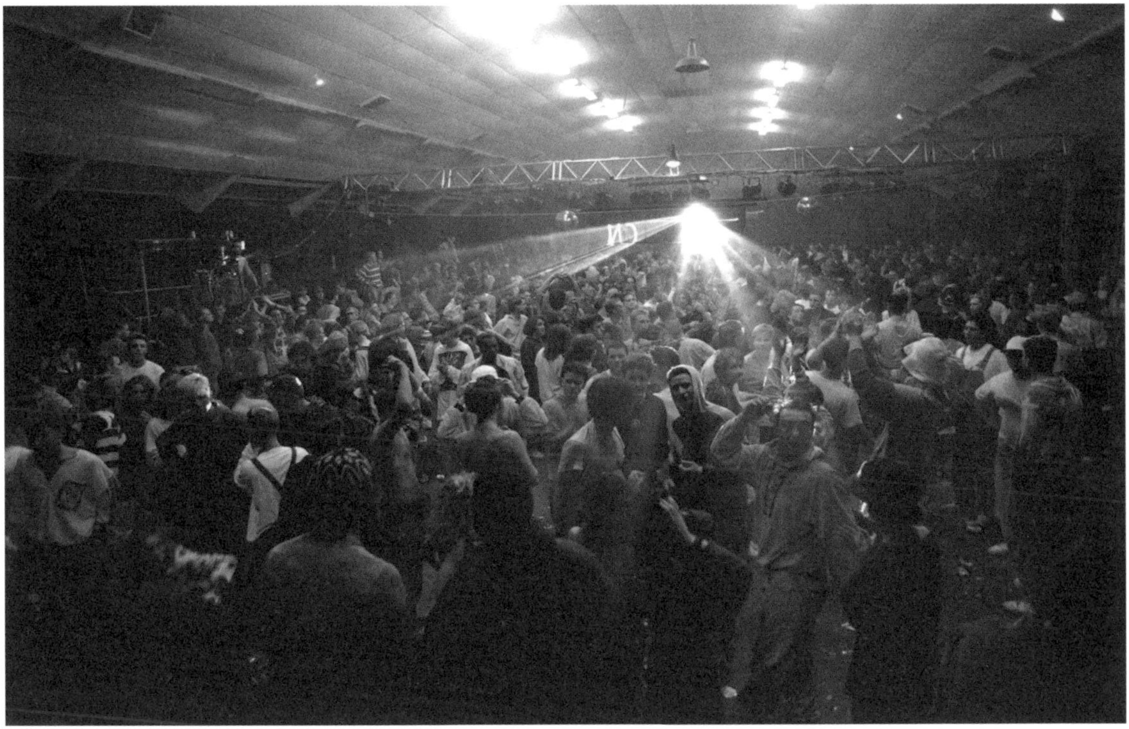

Fig. 11
Gavin Watson
Slough Centre, End of the Night
1989

Factories were a new world of moral chaos, extraordinary places, full of danger, where the youth of both sexes were often in heated proximity, deafened by the noise of the machines that shook the buildings and their bodies. Just the kind of experiences sought out and replicated in clubs and warehouse parties – parties that, for a short time in the late 1980s, took place in the same buildings where the machines and workers (possibly ancestors of the party's attendees) once laboured. The following passage reads like a tabloid editorial for the mid-Victorian era:

'The contagion of vicious example and impure conversation… compelled to make one of a society which is continually exhaling the miasma of vice… breathing its pollution every moment… The restless motion of the machinery has begun; the continual clack of the several wheels… There reigns in the work-rooms a Babel of confused sounds – the irreverent laugh, the open blasphemy, the licentious conversation… anger is stirred into acts of tyranny… In the heart of the factory – an assemblage of the vile of human beings, a fermenting mass of sin and vice, such as we may well doubt was ever before concentrated in one burning focus. It seems as if the mighty capacities of steam had lent an impetus, not only to the industry and ingenuity of man, but an equal impetus to all his faculties and contrivances of vice.'
— H. Worsley, *Juvenile Depravity*, 1849

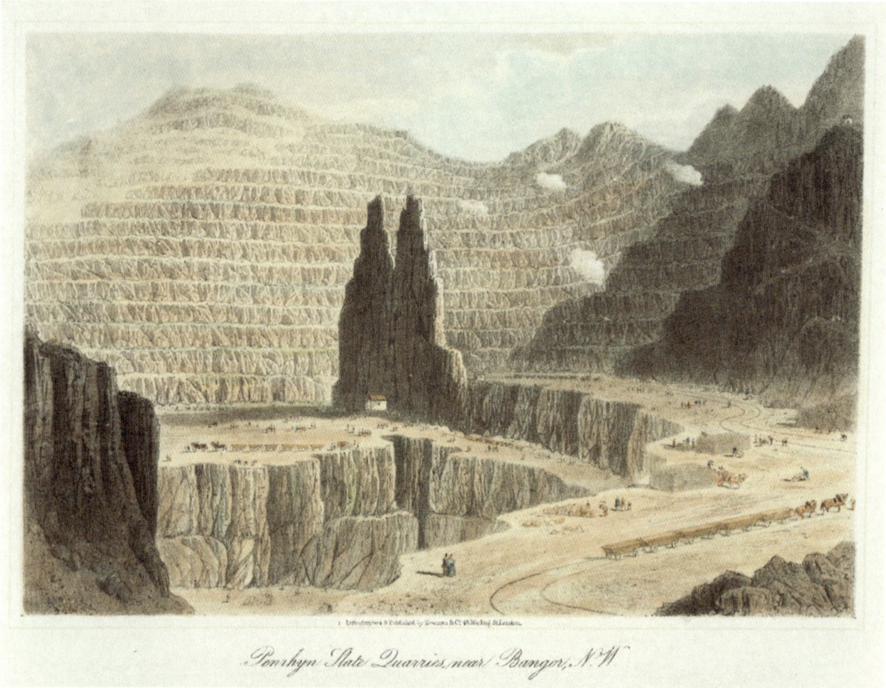

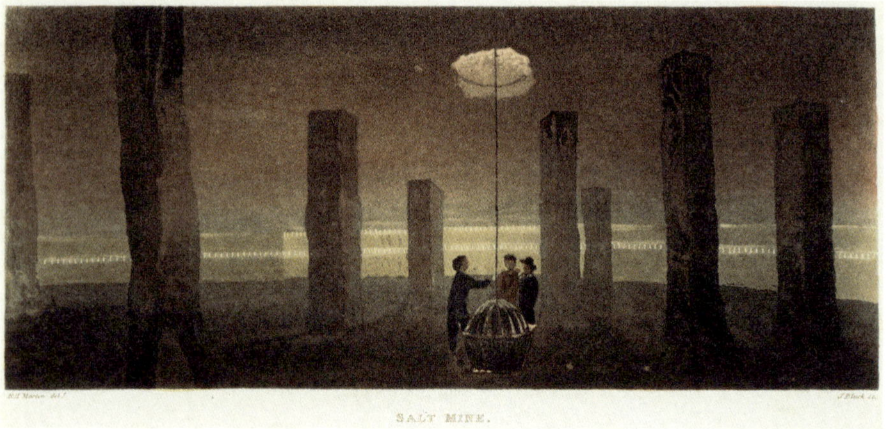

Fig. 12
Newman & Co
Penrhyn Slate Quarries, Near Bangor, Wales
1842

Fig. 13
Salt Mine, Cheshire
1814

Not all visions of the age were so negative or troubling. The epic interventions into nature by heavy industry were a gift to Romantic landscape artists. This was a moment when a salt mine became a temple and the Penrhyn Slate Quarry a Welsh Grand Canyon.

Fig. 14
Photograph of
James Sharples
Date unknown

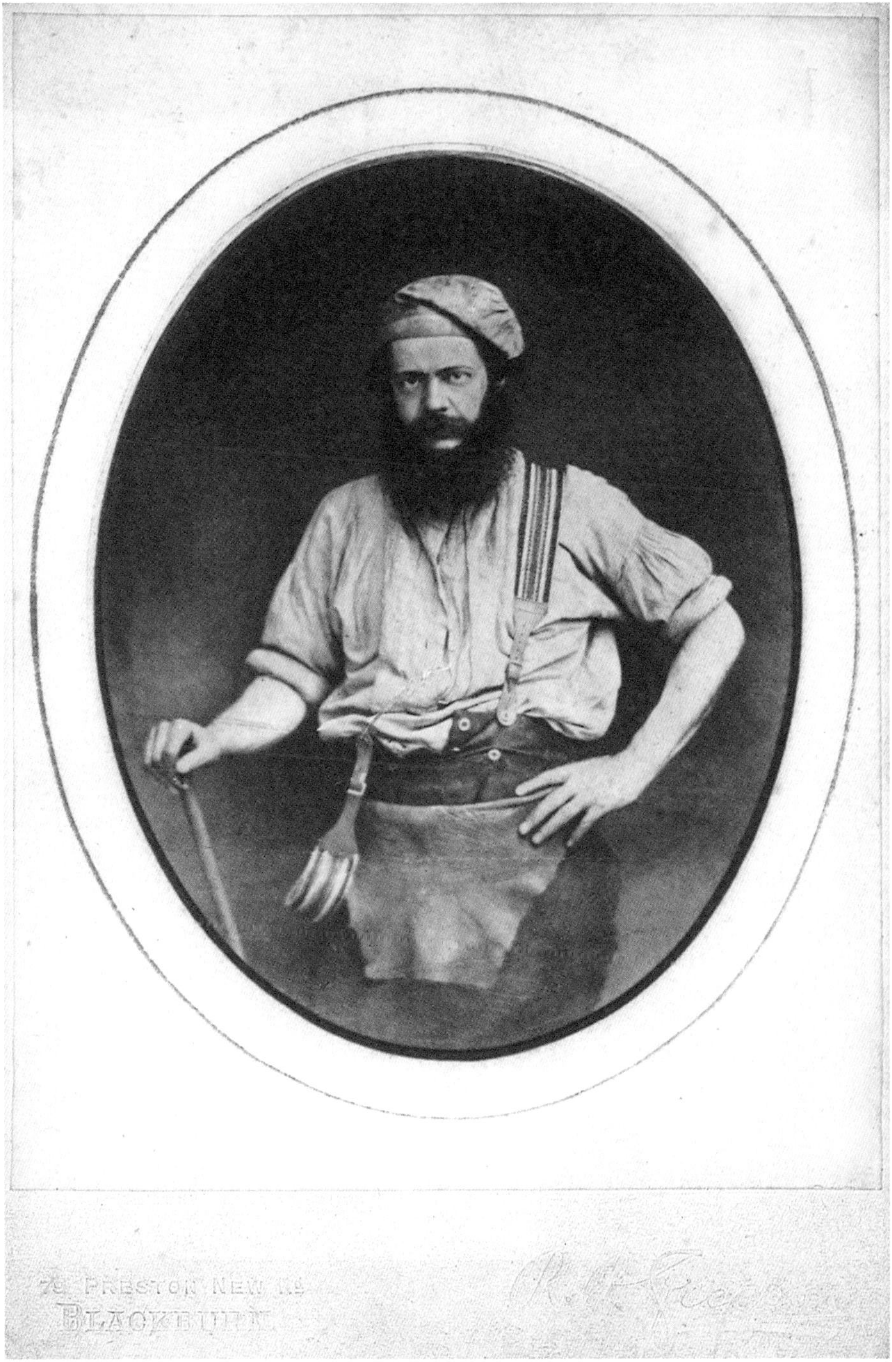

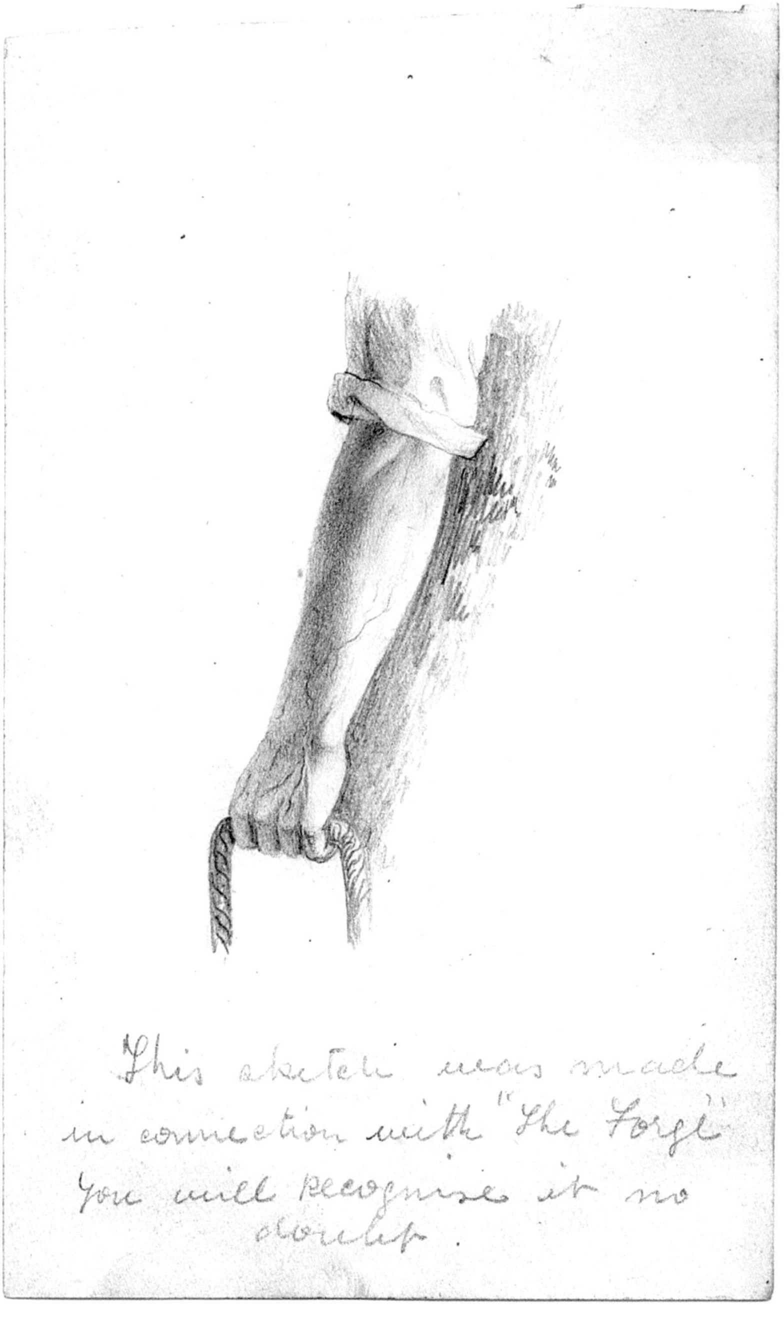

Fig. 15
James Sharples
Sketch of Forearm
for The Forge
Date unknown

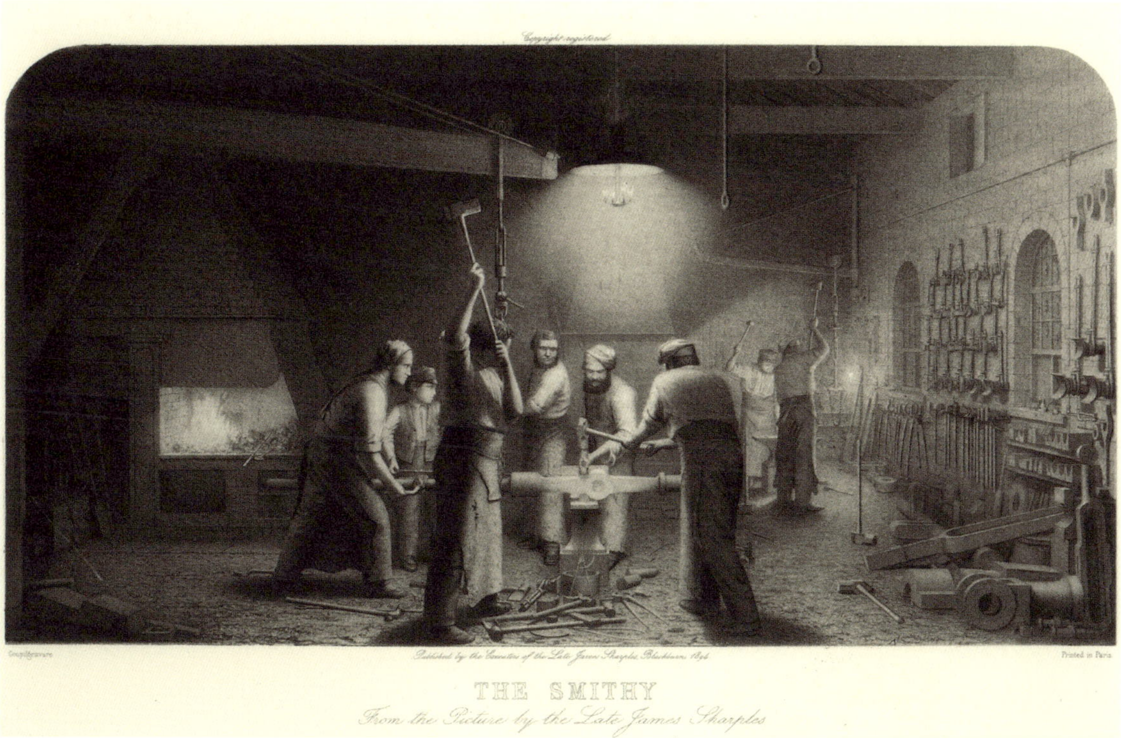

Factory life too was celebrated in the work of the self-taught artist James Sharples, posing on the previous page as an industrial worker. Sharples worked as a smith's boy in a foundry in Bury from the age of ten; at the age of 19 he began a painting entitled *The Forge* (1859), which he subsequently engraved, having spent ten years learning the technique. The print was a sensation: an industrial nativity scene, celebrating the birth of a piece of iron.

Sharples himself is an example of the 'self-help' philosophy popular with the emerging middle class of the time, which expounded that every man was the writer of his own destiny and that industry was a self-regulating pseudo-science that, left to itself, would ensure a harmonious balance for worker and factory / forge-owner alike. Despite this notion, and the print's popularity, he was never able to fully capitalise on his talent and had to remain in industry. He died a pauper in 1892.

Fig. 16
James Sharples
The Smithy
(reproduced after Sharples' death)
1894

With an iconography little changed from that exhibited in Sharples' work, Britain's post-war industrial rebirth was announced in *Steel* (1945). It was filmed by Jack Cardiff, a cinematic artist of light and shade, a John Martin or Joseph Wright for the twentieth century. Industry had never looked so good and would never look so good again. In the closing minutes, the stirring voiceover rallies a nation with its invocation of a shared industrial identity; poignant but for the wrong reasons:

'Britain is proud of her steel industry from the great record of output, quality and close understanding between workers and management has grown her name as producer of the world's finest steel. Making of this steel is something more than a skilled craft to the Jim Browns of Sheffield, the Jock McDonalds of Clydeside and the Bryn Evanses of South Wales. To them it is part of a long tradition, worthy of generations of craftsmen who have dedicated their life to steel, tough as these men who make it. An inspiration to the coming generation who will carry the flaming torch of Britain's steel industry. Making steel for the ships that plough the seven seas, steel for the planes that race across the skies, steel for the bridges and houses of a world at peace once more… Steel for the new life of tomorrow, that will reward the people of today.'

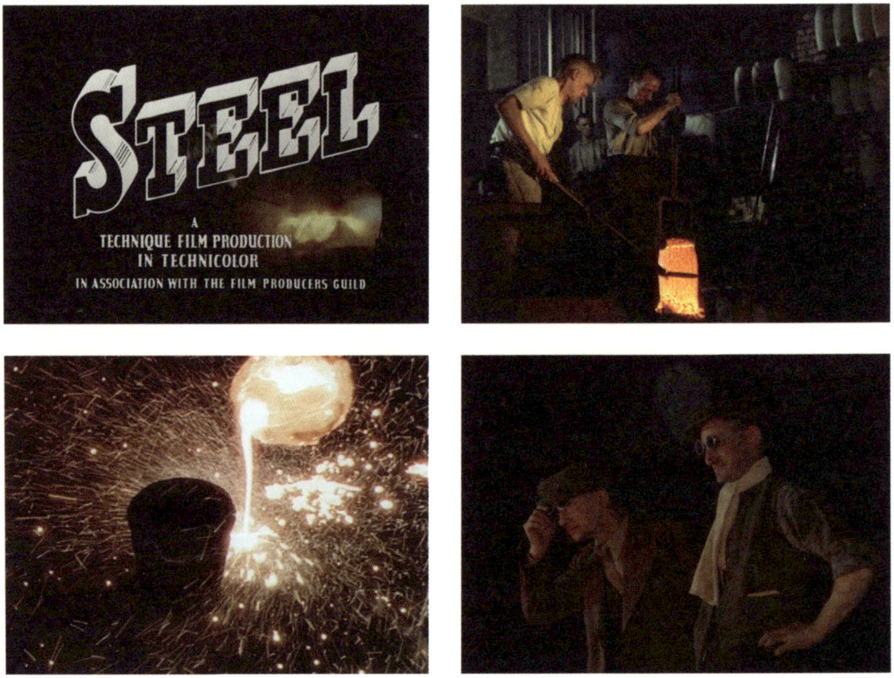

Fig. 17
Ronald Riley
(director),
Jack Cardiff
(cinematographer)
Steel
1945

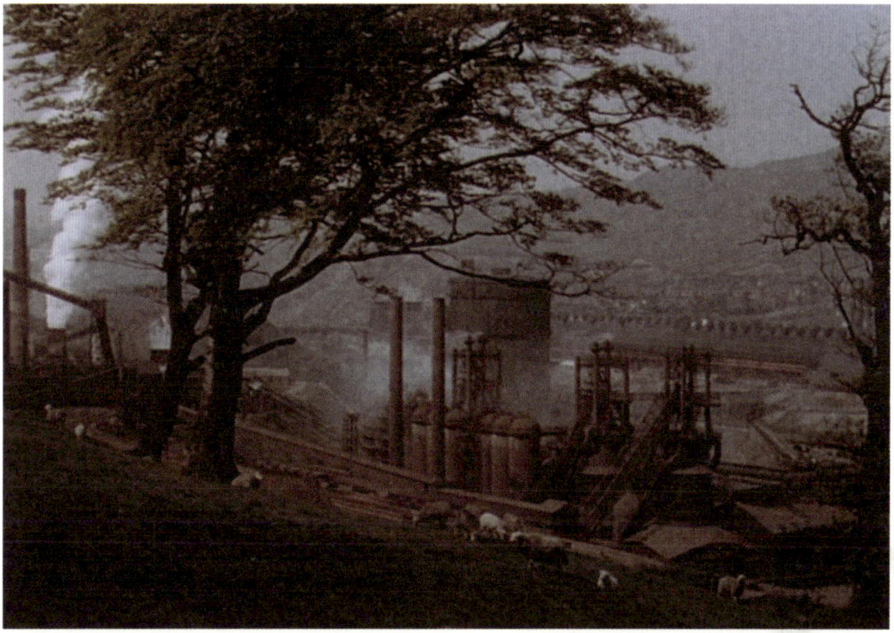

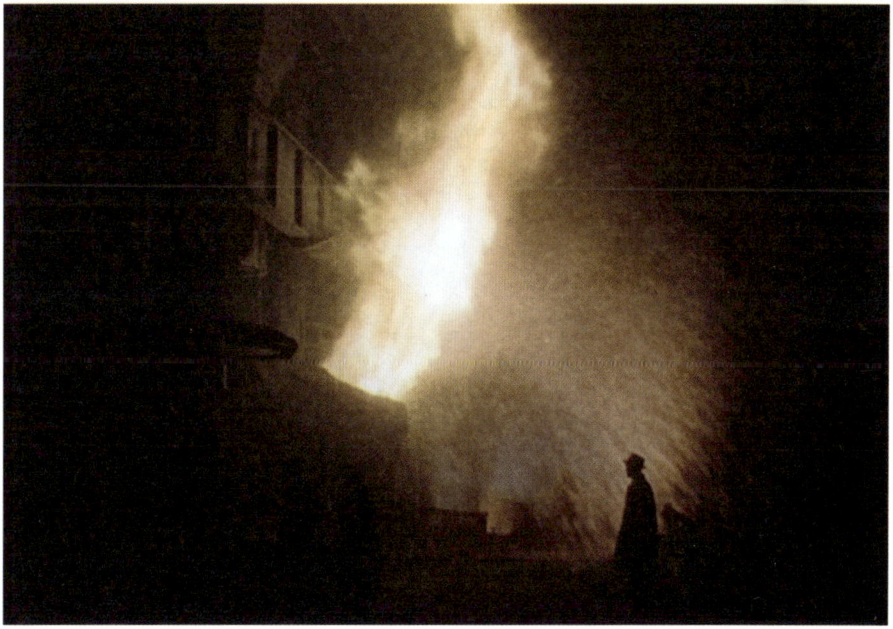

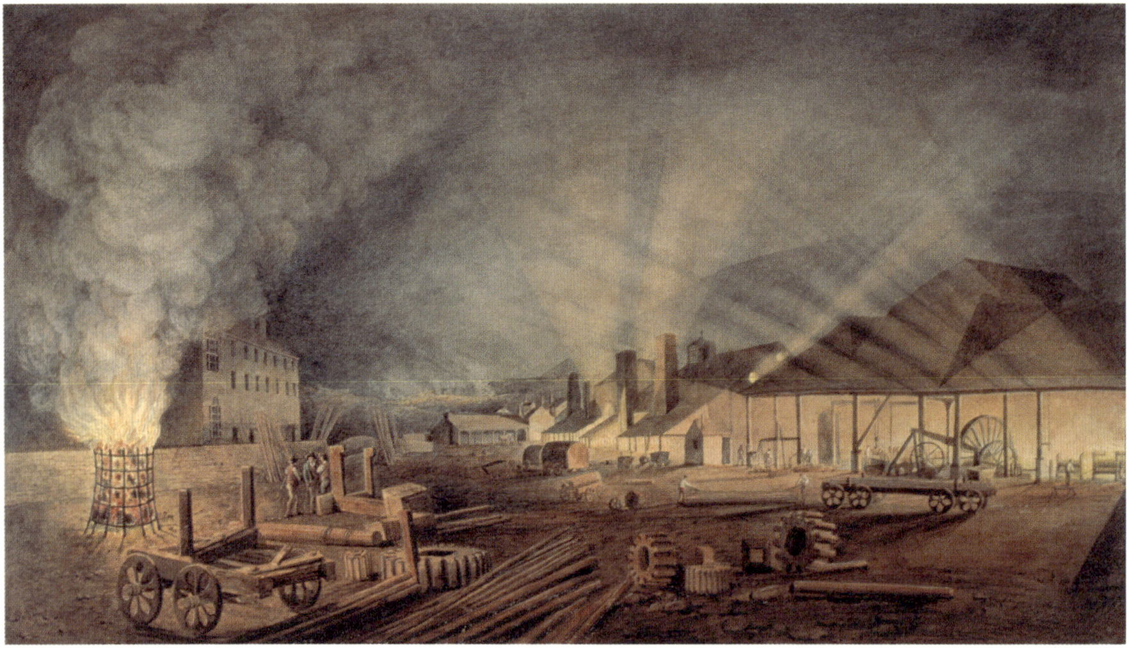

Thomas Hornor, an engineer, also understood the glamour of heavy industry. His depiction of the *Rolling Mills, Merthyr Tydfil* (1819) offers the kind of light show that would be emulated 160 years later by heavy metal bands. A music genre and a live experience that barely subconsciously celebrates an industry and culture through its sound and ritual. 'Metal' is both a re-enactment of an industrial process and a requiem for its loss. The music, like the industry, is in the blood – literally. Noddy Holder's family tree, for instance, is itself a history of the Black Country with relatives who were chain-makers, tong-filers and blacksmiths.

It has become something of a cliché to associate industrial sounds and rock music, but as this description of Birmingham from 1852 makes clear, it is an idea that has been around for 160 years:

'The people live in an atmosphere continually vibrating with clamour… it would seem as if their amusements had caught the general tone, and that the noises of the place, grown part of customary existence to its people – inwrought as it were, into the very staple of their lives – exerts over them some such unmarked influence as that exerted on the sleeper by the foundry; and that, when they relax from their labours, they seek to fill up the void by modulated noises, first caught up, like the song of the bird beside the cutler's wheel or coppersmith's shop, in unconscious rivalry of the clang of the hammers and engines.' — Hugh Miller, *First Impressions of England and its People*, 1847

Fig. 18
Thomas Hornor
Rolling Mills, Merthyr Tydfil
1819

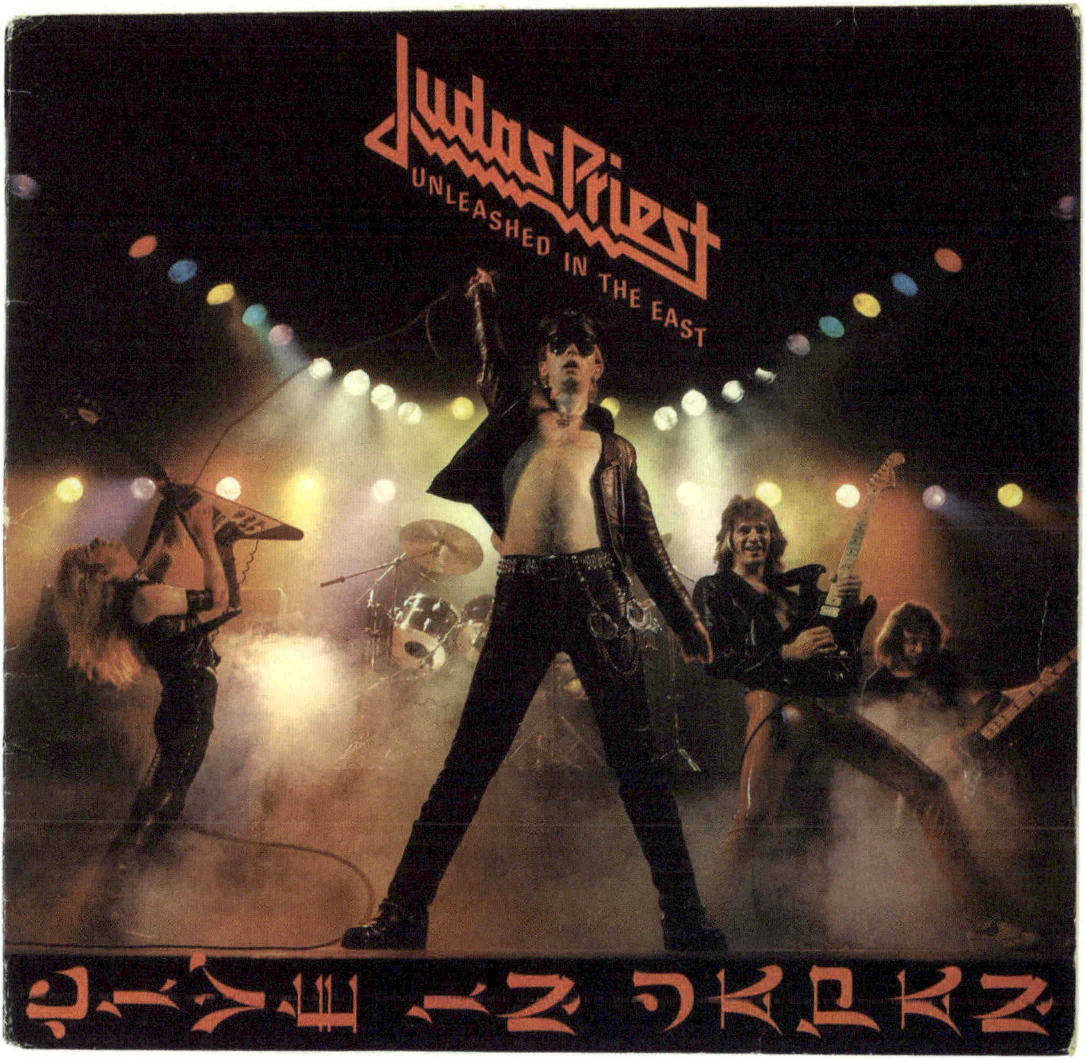

Fig. 19
Judas Priest
Unleashed in the East
1979

Bands like Judas Priest offered up a new form of masculinity to the de-industrialised youth of the UK – a look that would not have been out of place in a John Martin painting. For rock bands, the rigour of touring is a public declaration of their work ethic, turning something creative into a proper job.

The timed discipline of industrial work has musical implications, not only in terms of personal dedication, but also in the very heart of its regular, repetitive beat. When asked about how his sound related to his native Manchester, the record producer Martin Hannet recalled: 'I was struck years ago by a room full of air compressors in the Ferranti factory that were banging out this astonishing, four-in-the-bar bass-drum rhythm – I just stood in the centre of the room for hours.'

Fig. 20
REX/
Andre Csillag
Judas Priest – K K Downing, Dave Holland, Rob Halford, Ian Hill and Glenn Tipton, London
1981

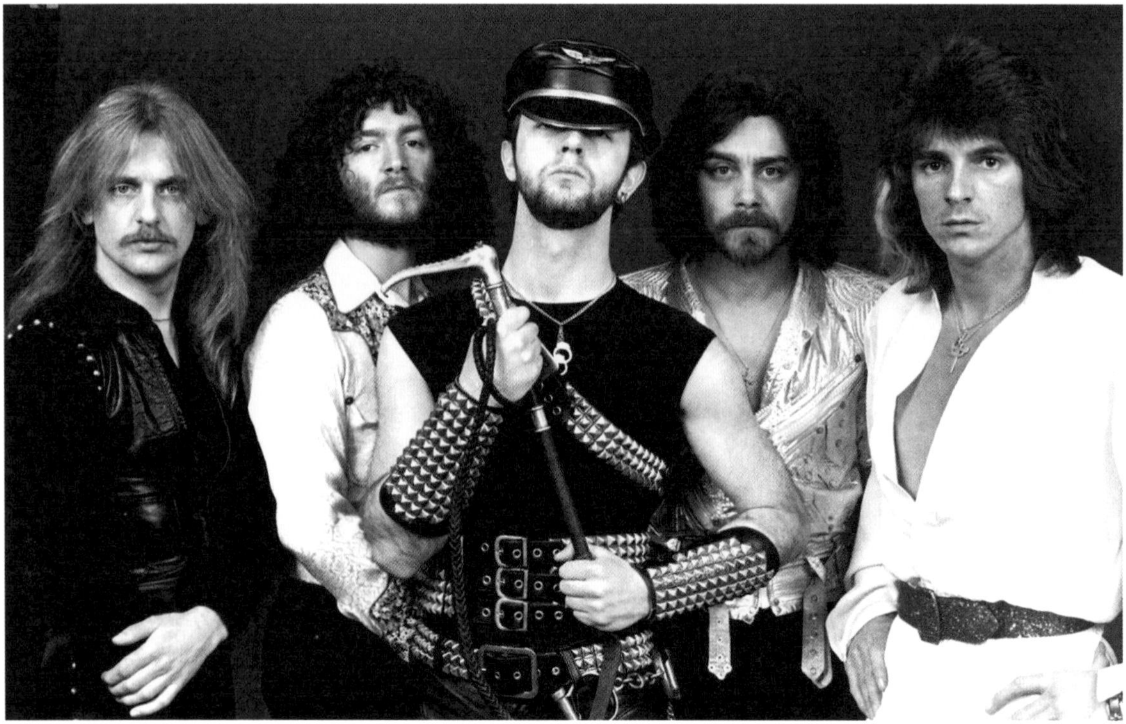

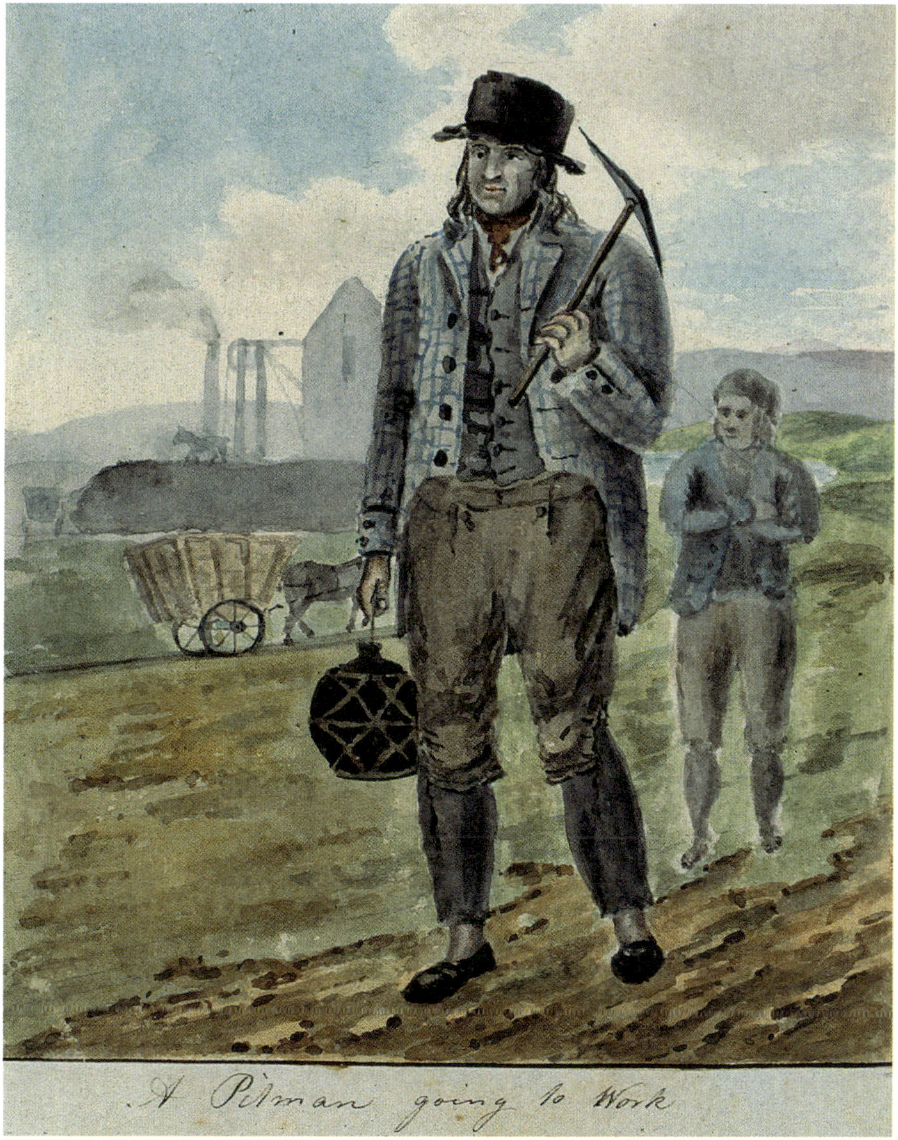

The sounds of mining are more mysterious, appropriate for an industry that mainly takes place out of sight. Miners of the nineteenth century were a breed apart – the industrial elite. Theirs was a tight-knit culture that pre-dated the Industrial Revolution. The image above shows a miner going to work – he would be unrecognisable on his return trip. The dangerous, subterranean working environment ensured better labour organisation with a stronger sense of their own worth than labourers in the newer industries; blackleg workers were dealt with harshly, even fatally on some occasions. Mining was harsh to an almost parodic degree; the following accounts of child labour are barely believable to a twenty-first-century reader.

Fig. 21
G. Jameson
A Pitman Going to Work
c. 1811

Fig. 22
Girl with Belt-and-Chain Dragging Coal Tubs Underground
Published in *Parliamentary Papers*
1842

'I have worked at this pit going two years. Coming to work at eight or before, but I set off from home at seven. I walk a mile and a half to my work, both in winter and summer. I get porridge for breakfast before I come, and bring my dinner with me – a muffin. When I have done about 12 loads I eat it while at work; I run 24 corves [coal wagons] a day; I cannot come up till I have done them all. If I want to relieve myself I go into any part of the pit. Sometimes the boys see me when they go by. My father slaps me sometimes upon the head, or upon the back, so as to make me cry.

'A very ignorant child (commented Mr. Scriven, the Sub-Commissioner), she stood shivering before me from cold. The rag that hung about her waist was once called a shift, which is as black as the coal she thrusts, and saturated with water, from the dripping of the roof and shaft. During my examination of her the banksman whom I had left in the pit came to the public-house and wanted to take her away, because, as he expressed himself, it was not *decent* that she should be (her person) *exposed* to us; oh no! It was criminal above ground; and like the two or three other colliers in the cabin, he became evidently mortified that these deeds of darkness should be brought to light.' — *Parliamentary Papers*, 1842, quoted in E. Royston Pike, *Human Documents of the Industrial Revolution in Britain*, 1970

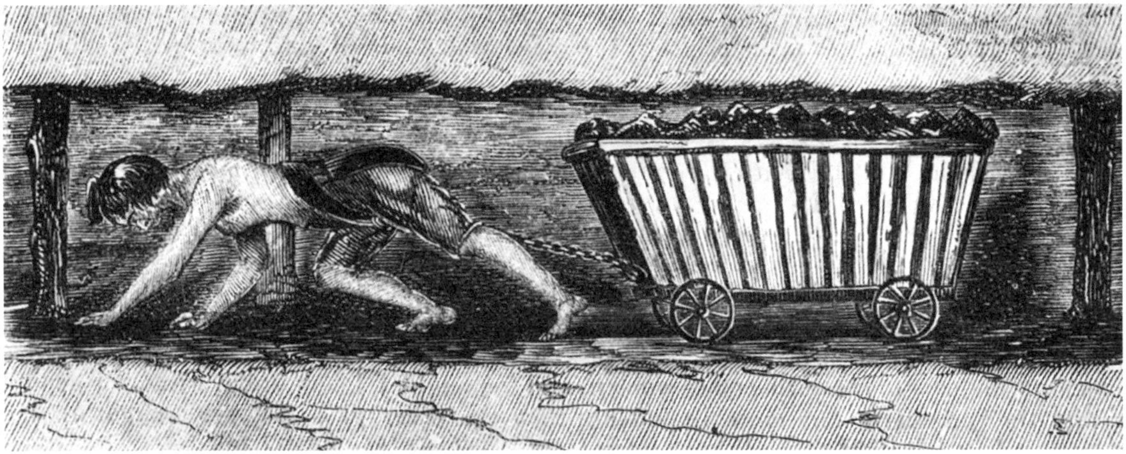

Fig. 23
Miner with Candle, Climbing Ladder
c. 1805

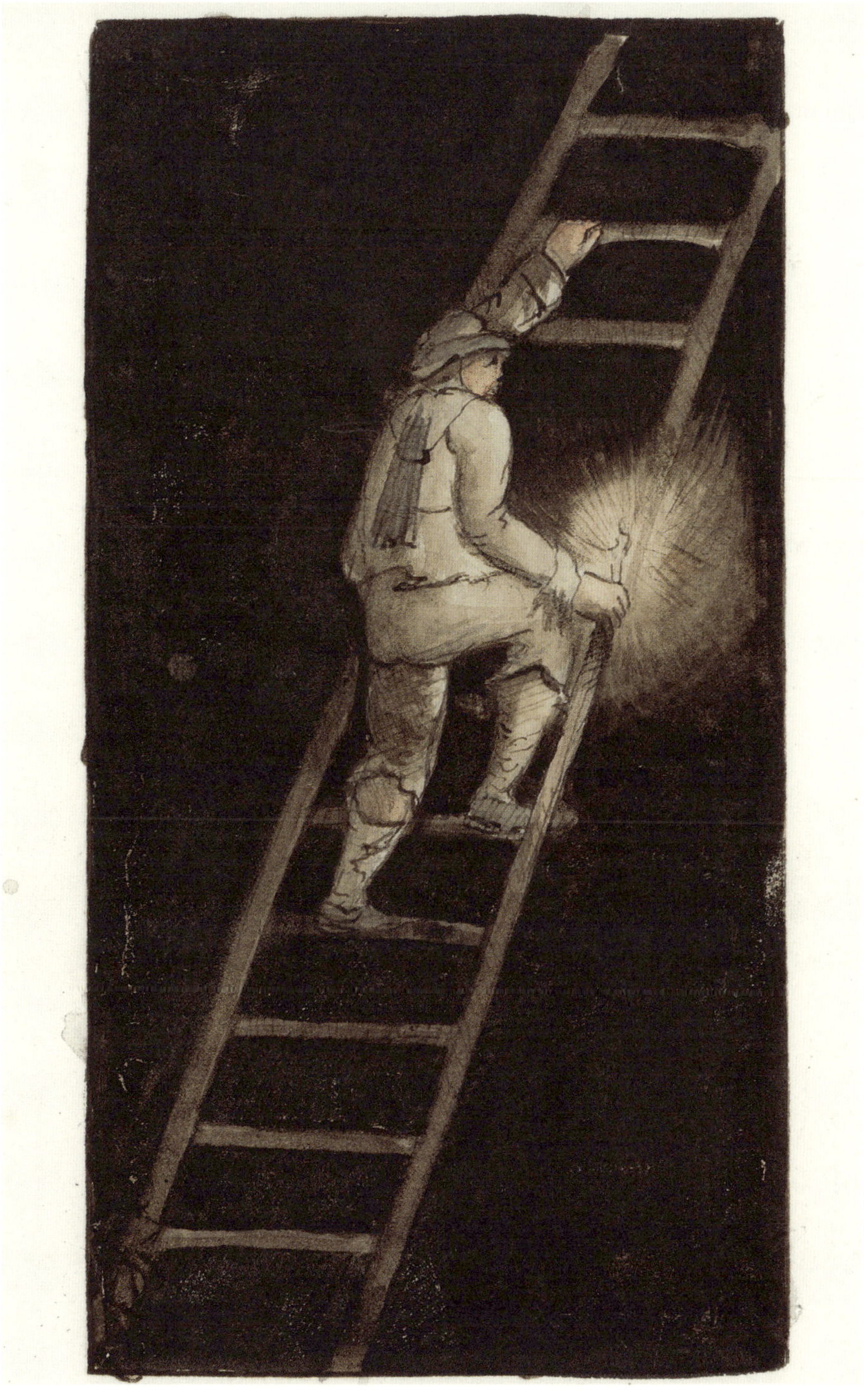

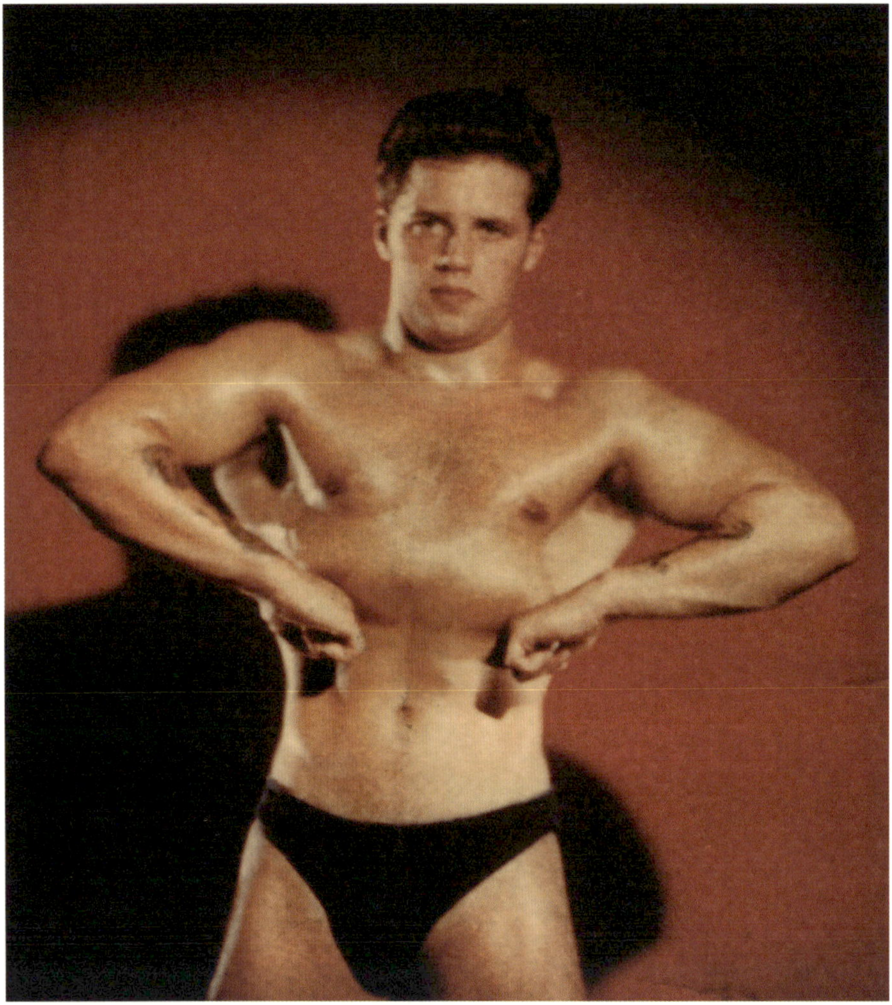

Fig. 24
Adrian Street
Bodybuilding
1975

Fig. 25
Adrian Street as Teddy Boy (second from right), *Wales* c. 1957

If James Sharples tried to leave a life of industrial toil by documenting it, Adrian Street (b. 1940) transcended it in a more spectacular fashion. When Street started work in a mine in 1955, children had been replaced by pit ponies, but the conditions at Brynmawr Colliery had not changed substantially. A keen bodybuilder, he left Wales for London at the age of 16, with the sound of jeering from his workmates and father ringing in his ears. Hanging around the Soho underworld he found success initially with body building and modeling. Seventeen years later he returned with his championship wrestling belts – part prodigal son, part prophet from the future, enlightening the coal serfs as to how the world would look in a post-industrial UK. The imagery is pure William Blake: the prophecy of Jerusalem has come to life as a shining Adrian lands to deliver us from industrial toil.

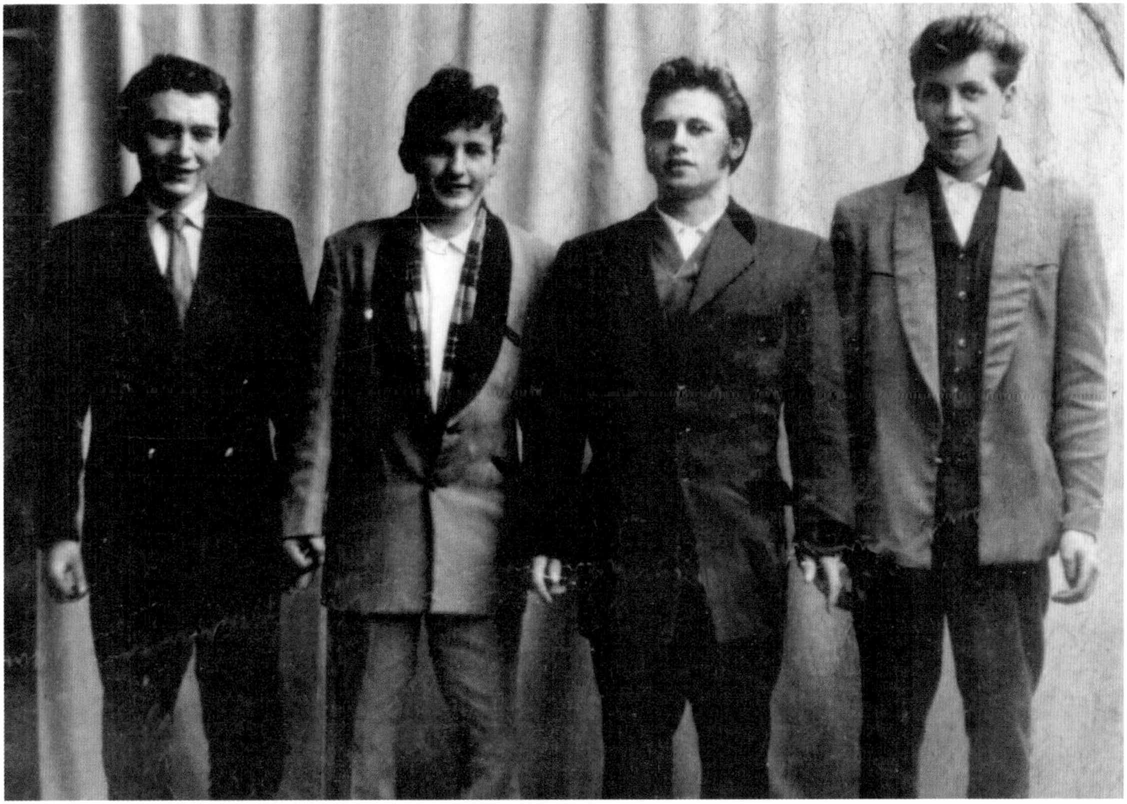

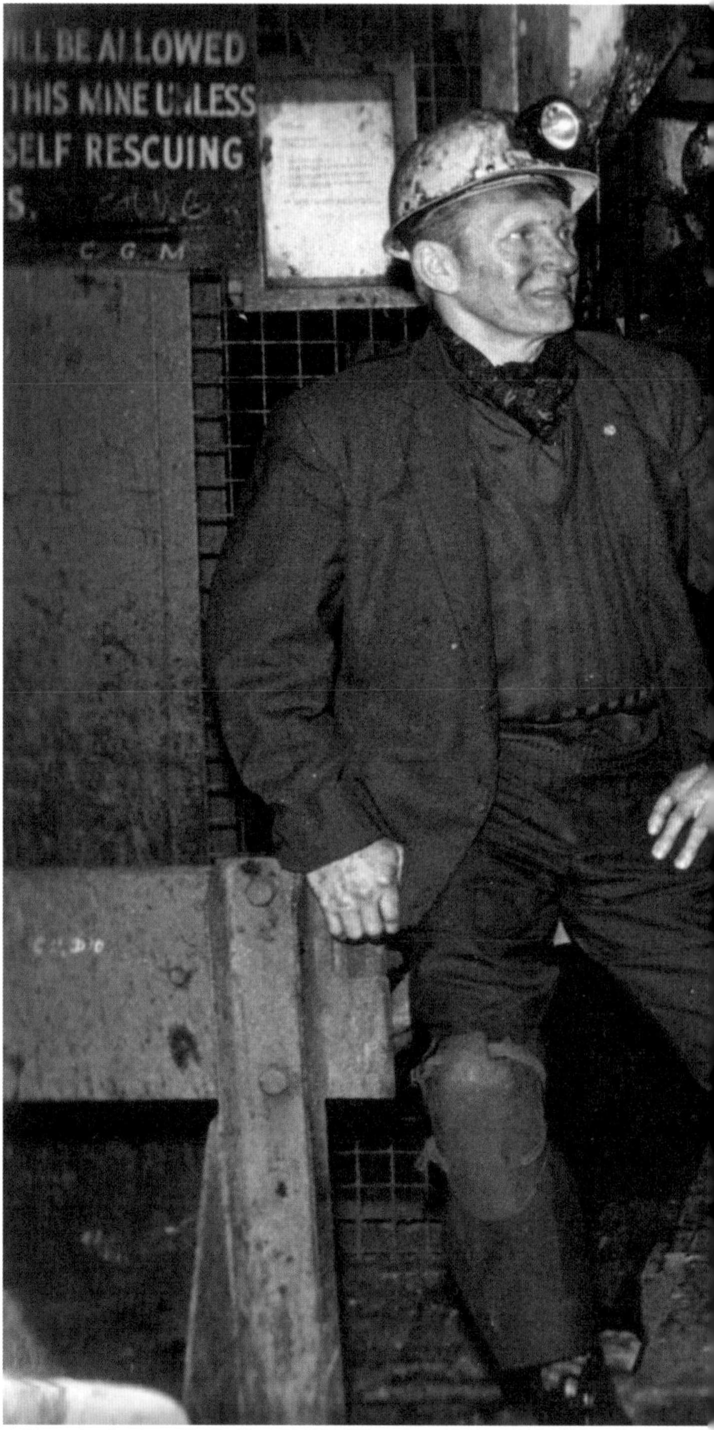

Fig. 26
Dennis
Hutchinson
Adrian Street
with his Father
at the Pithead
of Brynmawr
Colliery, Wales
1973

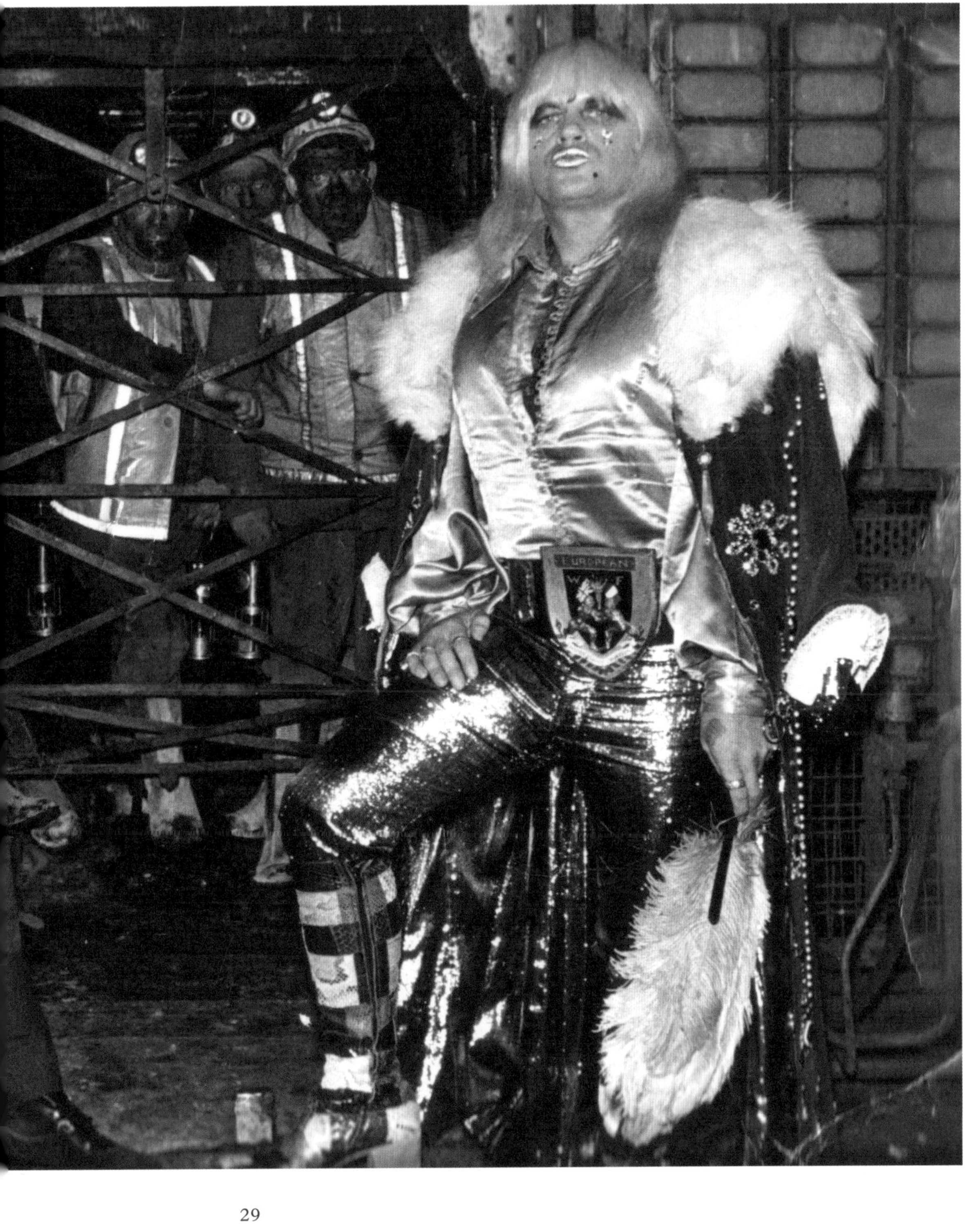
EUROPEAN

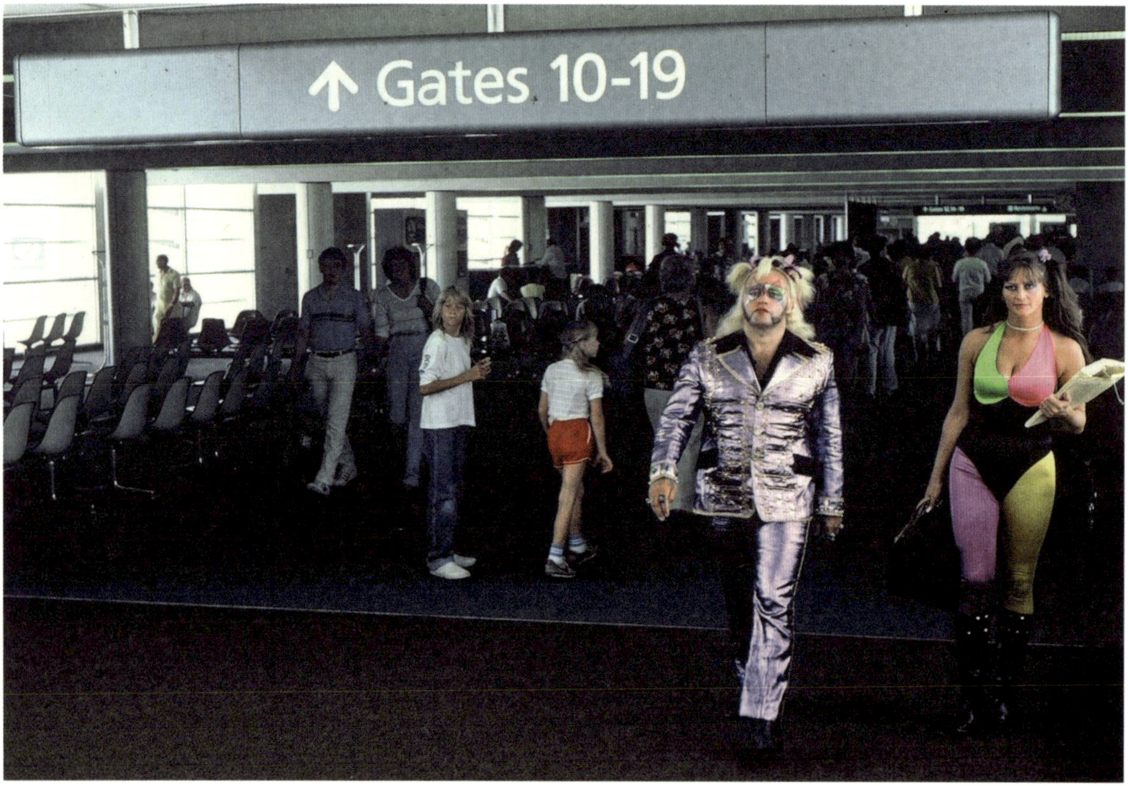

As with many pioneers, Street made up his destiny as he went along, influencing glam rock, fashion and, of course, his chosen trade, which he still occasionally indulges in. In 1980, wrestling was taken off TV in the UK, so Street left for the US where his outrageousness was amplified. Though shorter than most US wrestlers, he soon became a top attraction, introducing spandex and sexual ambiguity to the ring. He now has a cottage industry making costumes for wrestlers including all of those used in the film *The Wrestler* (2008). One of the few things that his profession had in common with factory life was the sound of the bell.

Fig. 27
Adrian Street at a US Airport with Valet, Miss Linda
Mid-1980s

Fig. 28
Adrian Wrestling in the UK
c. 1973

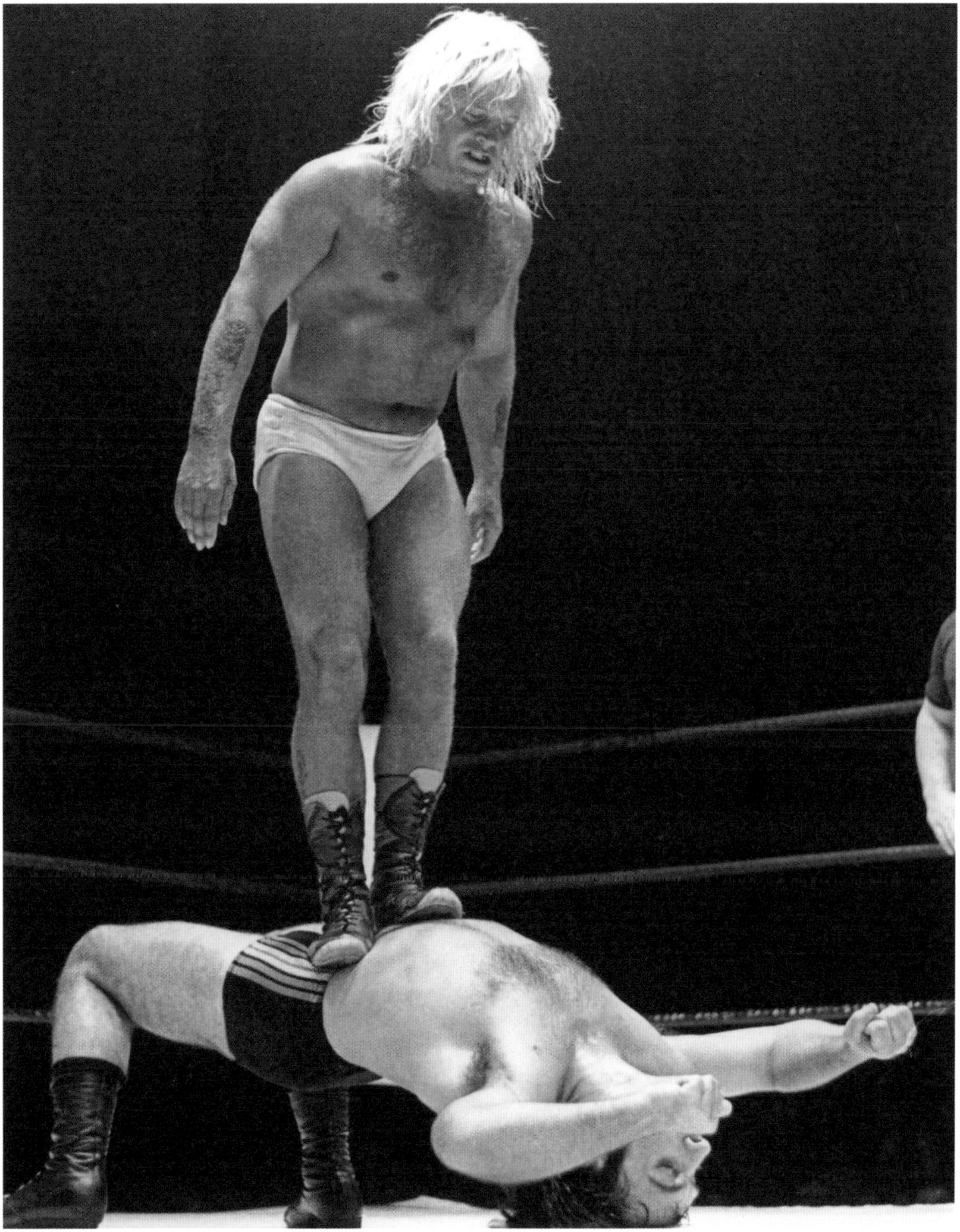

For the newly-industrialised Victorian factory worker, the fragmentation of time, coupled with what Friedrich Nietzsche called 'the endless repetition of the same' (first mentioned in *The Gay Science*, 1882), must have been a brutal shock to the system. No longer was time measured by the seasons and the rising and setting of the sun – 'time is nature' – now it was split into units of production, as humans became just another, potentially unreliable, part of a mechanical process.

'In reality there were no regular hours: masters and managers did with us as they liked. The clocks at the factories were often put forward in the morning and back at night, and instead of being instruments for the measurement of time, they were used as cloaks for cheatery and oppression. Though this was known amongst the hands, all were afraid to speak, and a workman then was afraid to carry a watch, as it was no uncommon event to dismiss any one who presumed to know too much about the science of horology.' — Anon, *Chapters in the Life of a Dundee Factory Boy*, 1887

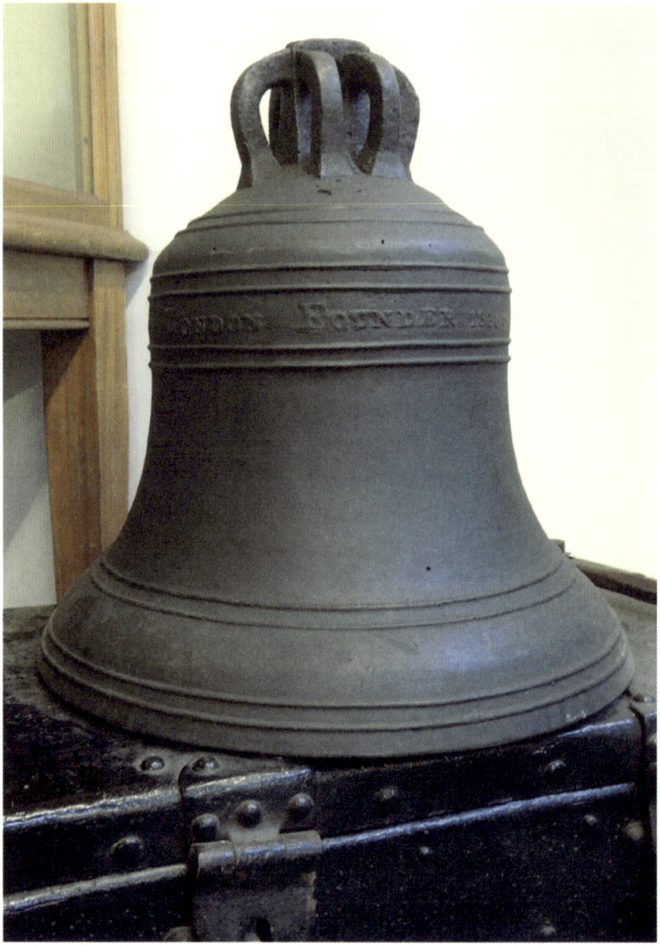

Fig. 29
Towers Yard Bell
1835

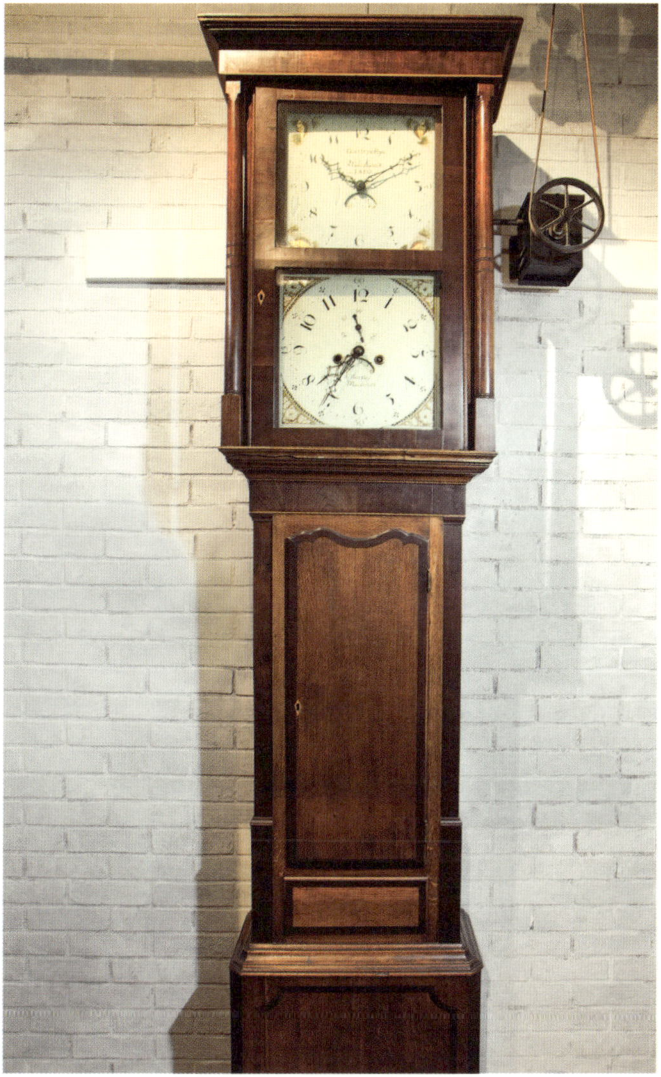

There were even clocks made that measured productivity as time: the two-faced timepiece shown here was connected to a watermill at a silk factory in Preston, and would show 'lost' time if the wheel did not turn quickly enough – this time would have to be made up at the end of the working day. Similar rules were not unusual in other factories: Crowley Ironworks had a rulebook that stretched to 100,000 words.

Fig. 30
E. Hartley
Double-Dial Longcase Clock from Green Silk Mill
1810

'In all these ways – by the division of labour; the supervision of labour; fines; bells and clocks; money incentives; preachings and schoolings; the suppression of fairs and sports – new labour habits were formed, and a new time-discipline was imposed…' — E. P. Thompson, *Work-Discipline and Industrial Capitalism*, 1967

Fig. 31
J. W. Lowry
Power Loom Factory of Thomas Robinson Esq., Stockport
1849–50

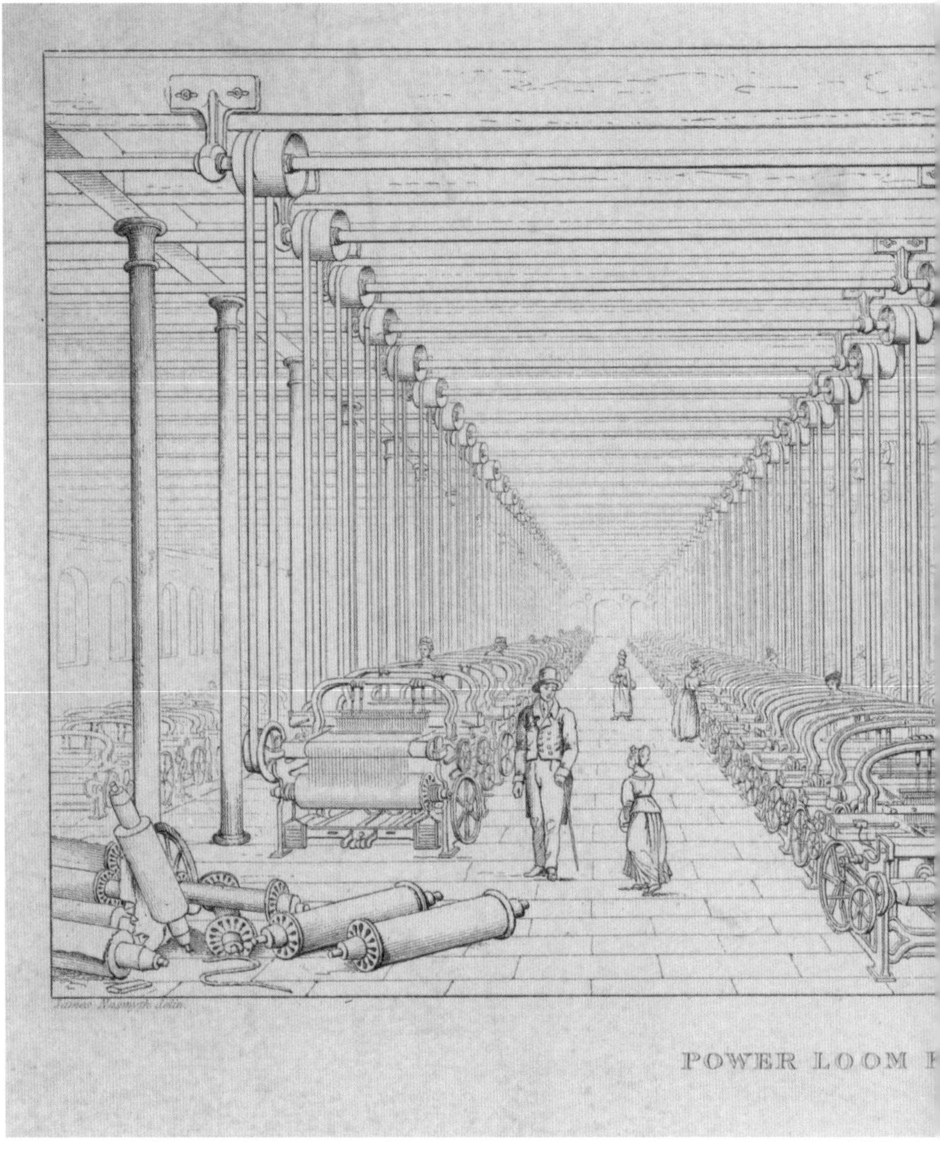

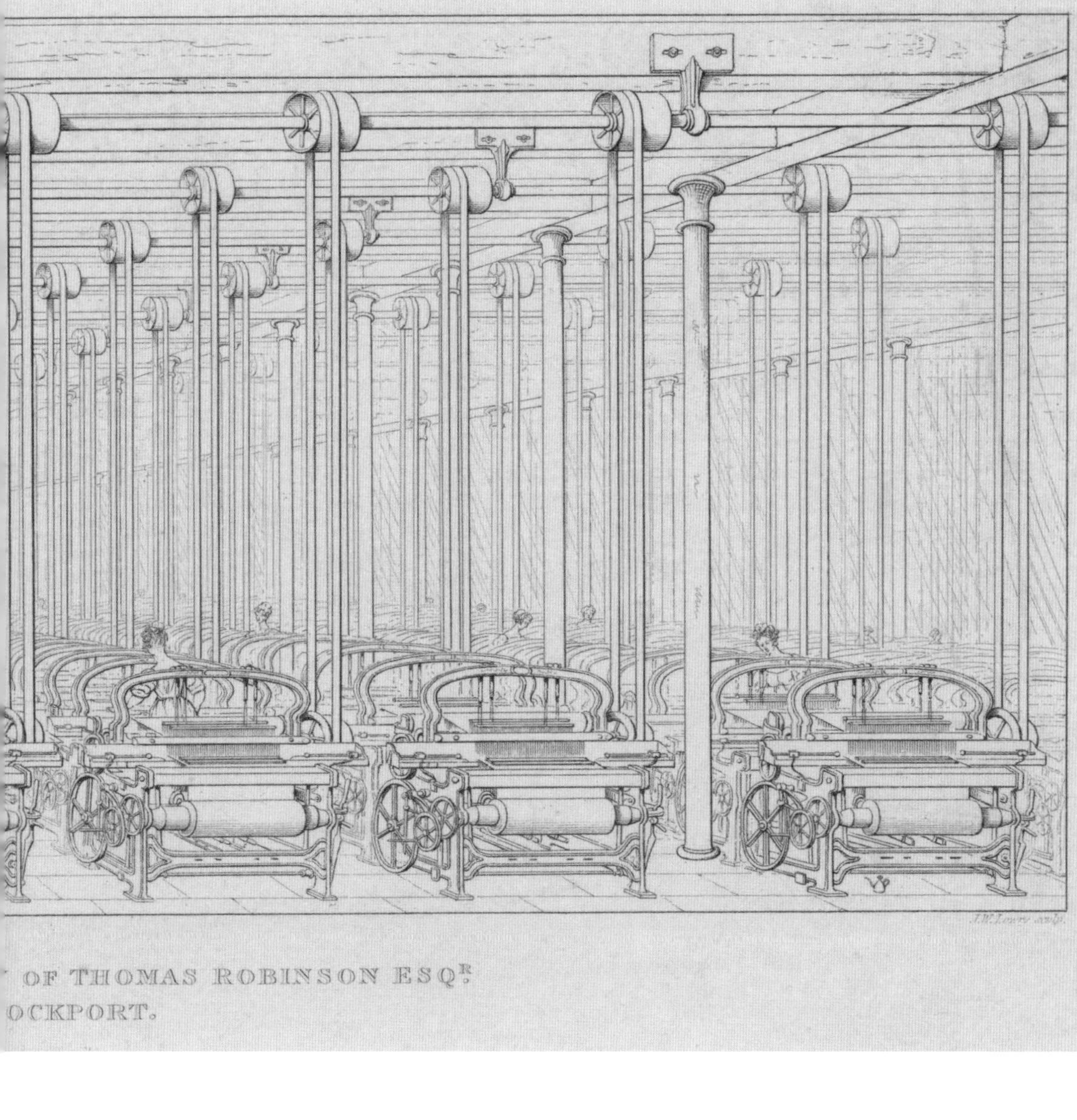

OF THOMAS ROBINSON ESQ^R.
OCKPORT.

Time discipline was often enforced with a complicated system of rules and fines, vividly illustrated in this poster from Thomas Ainsworth & Sons Mill in Preston. Many rules are based around subservience to the machine and its running, which, like the two-faced clock, is the true measure of time (Rules 3 and 4).

The 'necessary' in Rule 8 refers to the toilet, often a place of danger for women, as they were vulnerable to assault whilst there. Rule 9 forbids taking scraps of cotton into the toilet to use as loo roll. Trade unions were banned, which explains how Rule 1 could be enforced, whereby the worker had to give a least one month's notice, but could be sacked on the spot – another form of time discipline.

In 1853, a general strike amongst power-loom workers spread between mills in the North of England. 'The Preston Lockout' remained in place for the better part of eight months, during which time an estimated 20,000 to 26,000 workers were out of employment, half of them women and children. The strike was sparked by the disparity between the rising cost of living and pay, which was judged by strikers to be due a ten per cent increase.

The cartoon overleaf from the lock-out shows blackleg workers, known as 'knobsticks', being delivered and upacked for work. During the dispute, workers were banned from meeting in groups in the town and from singing protest songs, so would have meetings on the outskirts and sing songs like 'The Preston Steam Loom Weaver' and the rousing 'Ten Per Cent!' into the city:

'Come all you men of freedom, wherever you may be,
I pray you give attention, and listen unto me.
It's of this strike in Preston town, their courage being good,
I do believe they stand firm whilst they have life and blood
So now my boys, don't daunted be, but stand out to the fray:
We ne'er shall yield nor quit the field, until we've won the day.'

Fig. 32
Thomas Ainsworth & Sons
Rules to Be Observed in this Factory, Church Street Mills, Preston
c. 1830

RULES

TO BE OBSERVED

And kept by the People

EMPLOYED IN THIS FACTORY.

1st.

EACH Person employed in this Factory engages to serve **THOMAS AINSWORTH and SONS**, and to give one Month's Notice, in writing, previous to leaving his or her employment, such notice to be given in on a Saturday, and on no other day; but the Masters have full power to discharge any Person employed therein without any previous Notice whatsoever.

2nd.

THE hours of attendance are from Six o'clock in the Morning until half-past Seven at Night, excepting Saturday, when work shall cease at half-past Four; half an hour allowed for Breakfast, and one hour for Dinner; and any Person not coming to work at the stated periods shall for every offence, forfeit Sixpence, and be deducted for the time they are absent.

3rd.

ALL Wages (to be calculated according to the time the Steam Engine may have run) shall be due and payable on each Saturday, in the Afternoon, one hour after the same shall have been demanded at the Counting-house, by the Person or Persons entitled thereto; and in no case whatsoever shall they be due or payable at any other time; and any Person leaving his or her employment without notice, shall forfeit all wages due at the time at which he or she left such employment.

4th.

ANY Spinner whose wheel or wheels are standing either for want of Piecers or from any other cause whatsoever, during the time the Steam Engine is going, or not keeping them employed at their usual and proper speed, shall, for every hour, pay sixpence.

5th.

EACH Spinner shall keep his or her wheels and wheel-house clean swept and fluked, or in default thereof, shall forfeit One Shilling.

6th.

IF any waste, rovings, utensils, or machinery of any kind be misused, spoiled, damaged, lost, or carelessly misplaced, the Person so misusing, spoiling, damaging, losing, or carelessly misplacing the same, shall forfeit and pay One Shilling; and also pay the value thereof, if lost, spoiled, or damaged.

7th.

ANY Person altering in any way whatever the wheels or other machinery at which he or she is employed, or permitting the same to be done (without leave from a Proprietor or Overlooker) shall for every offence, forfeit Five Shillings.

8th.

EACH Person shall clean the Necessary belonging to the room in which he or she is employed, when thereunto required by the Overlooker; and any one neglecting or refusing so to do, or wilfully dirtying the same, or any part of the Factory, Yard, or adjoining Grounds, shall forfeit 2s. 6d.

9th.

ANY Person taking cotton or waste into the Necessaries, shall forfeit Two Shillings and Sixpence; and any one knowing of the same, and not giving information thereof, shall forfeit Five Shillings.

10th.

ANY Person smoking Tobacco, or having a pipe for that purpose, in any part of the Factory or Yard, shall forfeit Five Shillings.

11th.

ANY Person (excepting those specially appointed for that purpose) lighting the Gas, shall, for each offence, forfeit One Shilling.

12th.

ANY Person introducing a Stranger into the Factory without leave of one of the Proprietors, shall forfeit Two Shillings and Sixpence; and any Overlooker neglecting immediately to order such Stranger out, shall forfeit Five Shillings.

13th.

ANY Person or Persons neglecting thoroughly to clean the machinery under their care, when required by an Overlooker so to do, shall forfeit Two Shillings and Sixpence.

14th.

ANY Person temporarily leaving the frame at which he or she ought to be employed, or in any way neglecting his or her employment, shall forfeit One Shilling.

15th.

ANY Person taking tools out of the Mechanics' or Overlookers' Rooms, except the Mechanics or Overlookers themselves, shall forfeit Two Shillings and Sixpence.

16th.

WHEN any window or windows shall be broken, the party breaking the same shall pay the damage; but if the said party cannot be identified, the charges of repairing the the same shall be borne equally amongst all the Persons working in the room in which the said window or windows shall be so broken.

17th.

ANY Workman coming into the Factory, or any other part of these Premises, drunk, shall pay Five Shillings.

18th.

EACH Person employed in this Factory, engages not to be a member of, or directly or indirectly a subscriber to, or a supporter of, any Trades Union, or other Association whatsoever (the regular and legal Sick Clubs alone excepted.)

19th.

ANY Person destroying or damaging this Paper, shall pay Five Shillings.

20th.

TO avoid any misunderstanding or disputes, it is hereby determined, that when a breach has been made in any of the foregoing Rules, and the Person committing the same cannot be identified, double the penalty hereby inflicted shall be taken from the People employed in the department where the fault has been committed, whether it may extend only to one room, one Overlooker's department, or the whole Factory. And that all the above Payments, Fines, and Penalties shall be deducted out of the offenders' wages.

PRITT, PRINTER, 29, FISHERGATE, PRESTON.

Fig. 33
Preston Lock-Out
1853

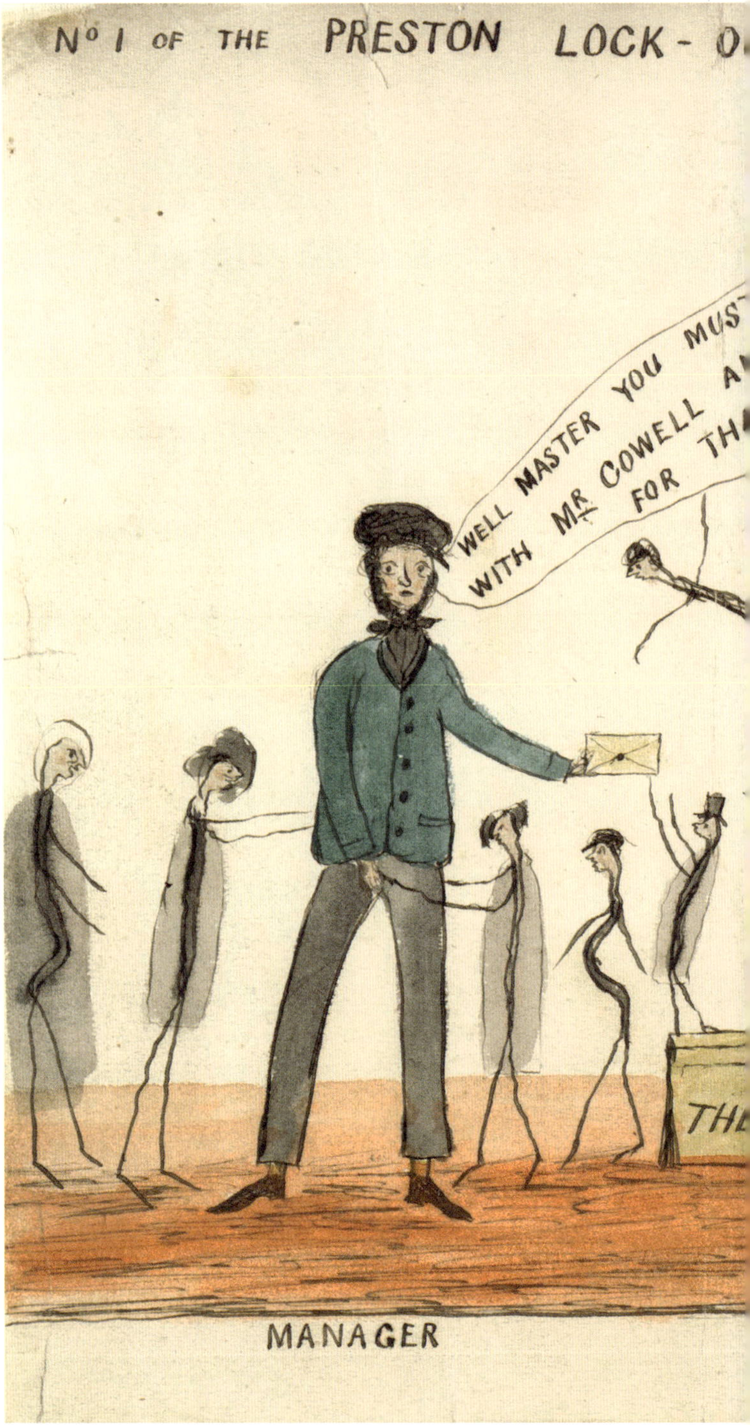

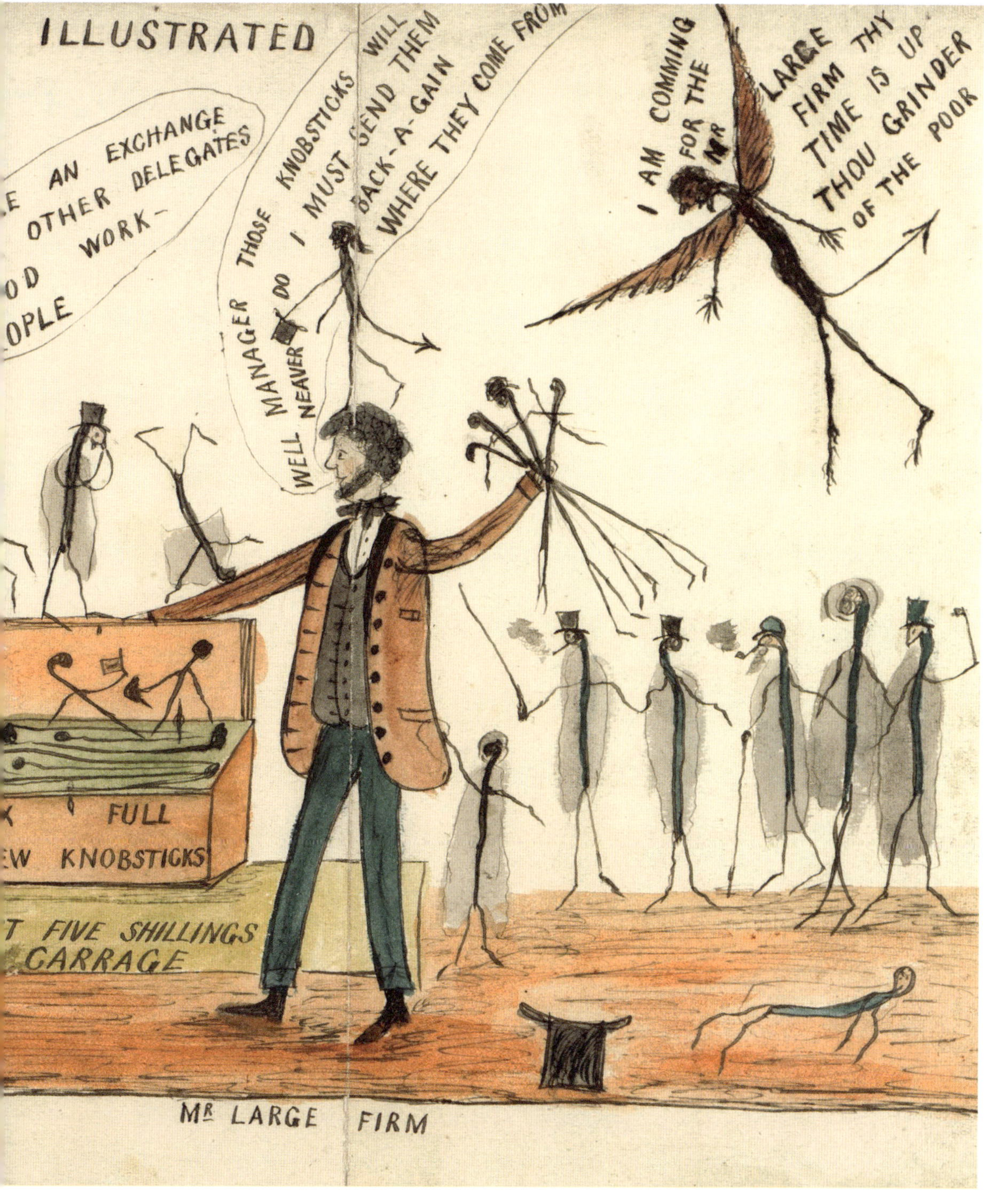
ILLUSTRATED
E AN EXCHANGE OTHER DELEGATES OD WORK- OPLE
WELL MANAGER THOSE KNOBSTICKS WILL NEAVER DO I MUST SEND THEM BACK-A-GAIN WHERE THEY COME FROM
I AM COMMING FOR THE MR LARGE FIRM THY TIME IS UP THOU GRINDER OF THE POOR
FULL
EW KNOBSTICKS
T FIVE SHILLINGS
GARRAGE
MR LARGE FIRM

It is no surprise that time became known as 'the enemy', as in 'how's the enemy?' – 'what time is it?' The item most often saved up for by miners was a pocket watch. By the same token, victories over time were hard won and energetically celebrated; this 1890 Amalgamated Engineers' Union banner from Newcastle celebrates a reduction by one hour of the working week. The progressive shortening of the working week is one of the key ways that organised labour could demonstrate its effectiveness.

The phrase opposite is the content of a text message sent to a zero-hours worker, informing him that his labour would not be required on the day in question. It is thought that as many as one million people in the UK are currently working on zero-hours contracts: employment agreements that give the worker no guarantee of shifts or of regular work patterns in any given week. The worker is effectively on call and there is no obligation for the employer to provide sick or holiday pay. While this kind of contract offers a certain amount of flexibility, the advantage is largely on the side of the employer, making it very difficult for the employee to plan and control their finances, creating a new form of day labouring in the service and digital economies.

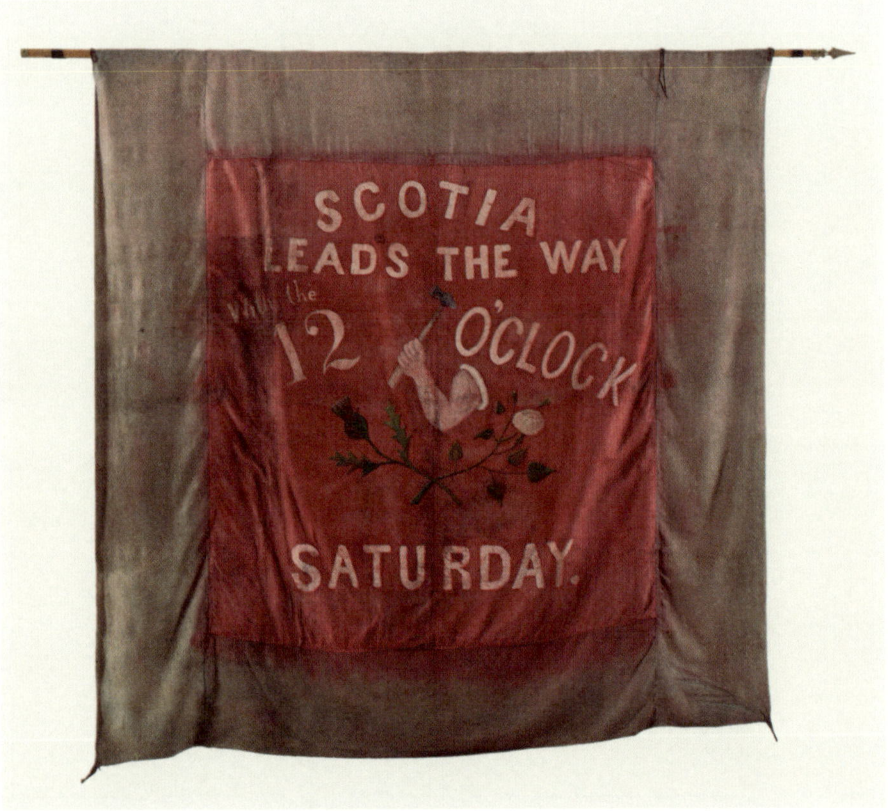

Fig. 34
Amalgamated Engineers Union Banner
1890

Hello,
Today you
have
day off

Fig. 35
Text Message to Worker on a Zero-Hours Contract
2013

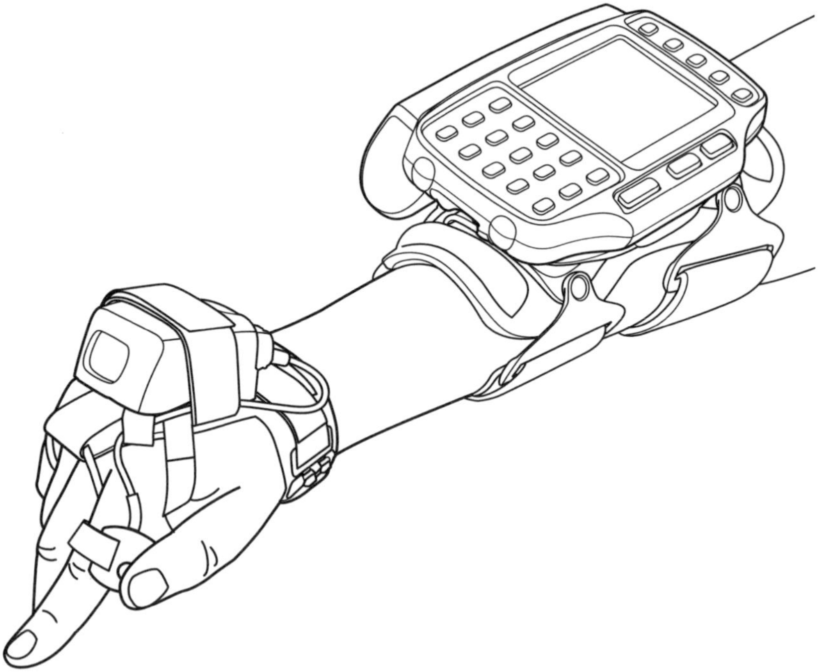

Many zero-hours contracts are for low-wage work in warehouses, where a further time discipline is enforced by productivity devices, like the Motorola WT4000: a tracking device designed to increase productivity and reduce errors. Worn on the wrist, the device informs the worker where to go and what to do and will also track how fast tasks are completed, sending the worker messages to speed up as the system considers necessary. The sheer scale of the Amazon warehouse in Rugeley, Staffordshire, where similar devices are used, would no doubt have impressed John Martin.

'The rooms are all crowded with dangerous machinery; so close that you can hardly pass... Not any of this machinery is boxed off, or guarded in any way. It is a frightful place, turn which way you will. There is a constant hammering roar of wheels, so that you could not possibly hear any warning voice...' — Richard Hengist Home, *Report of the Royal Commission on Children's Employment in Mines and Factories*, 1842

Fig. 36
Motorola WT4000 Wearable Terminal
2013

Fig. 37
Ben Roberts
Amazon Fulfilment Centre, Towers Business Park, Rugeley
2013

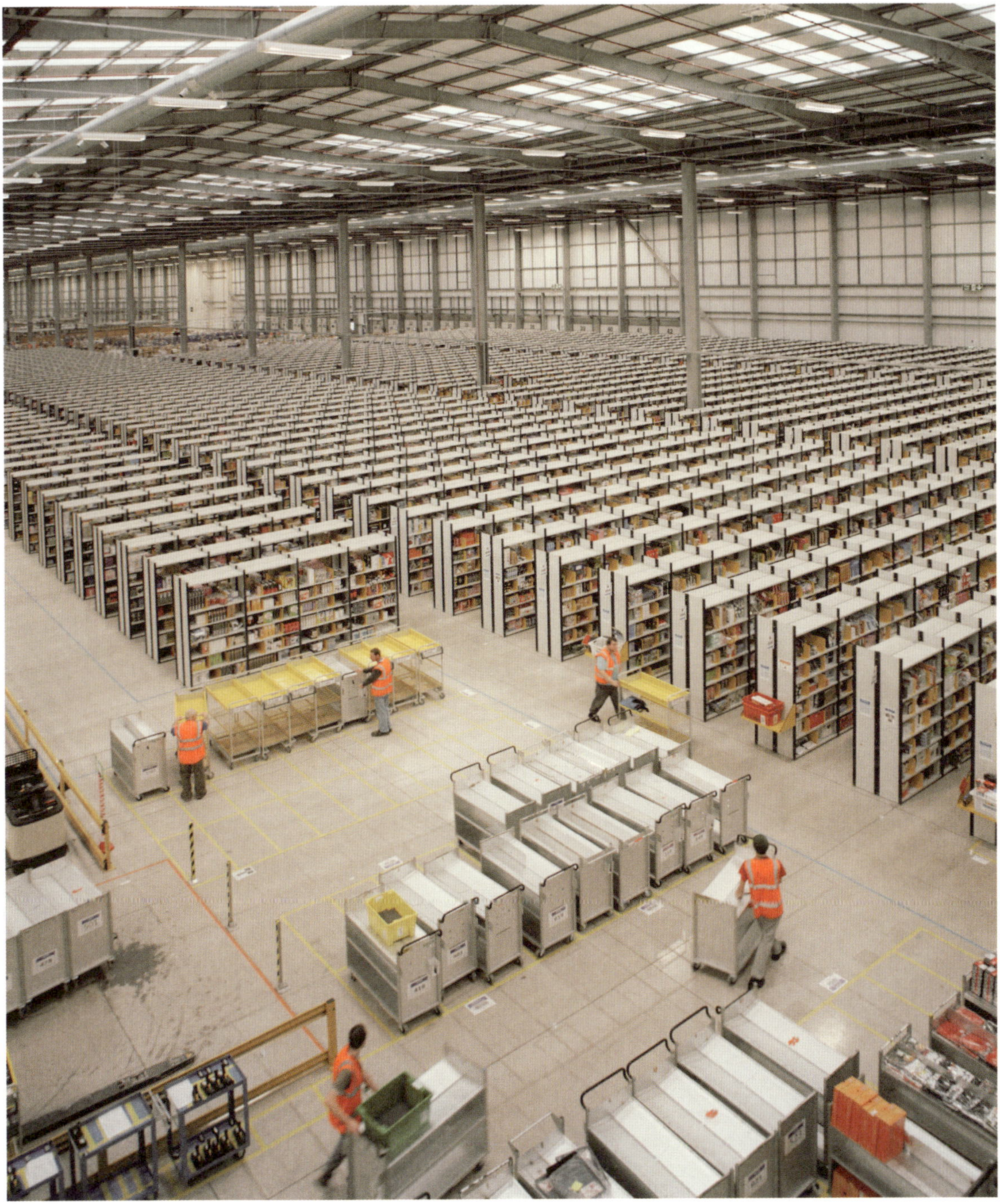

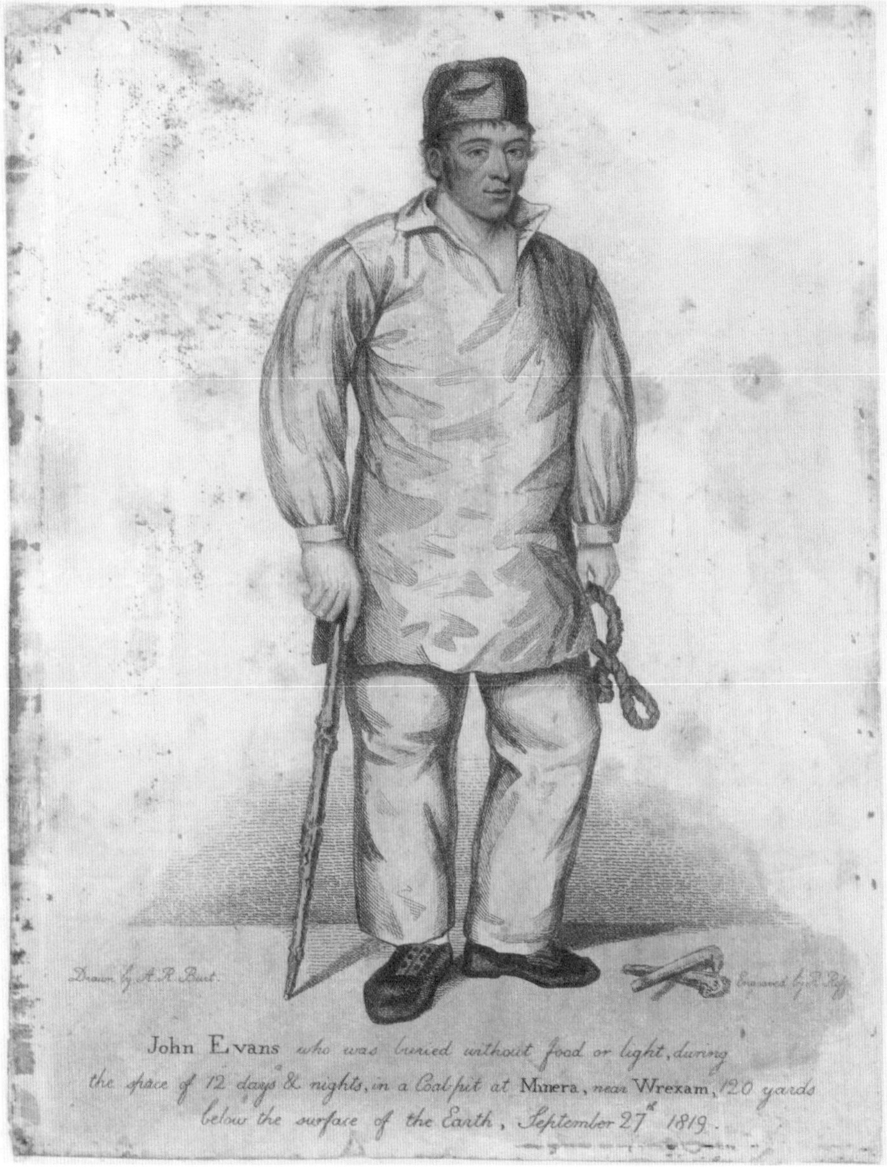

In the working environment discipline was imposed as much by the ever-present threat of injury as by any positive actions of employers, and these dangers were not insignificant. The miner John Evans was trapped underground for 12 days after a mine collapse at Wrexham in Wales, in 1819; he survived by eating candles and drinking mine water and was pulled out in a delirious state. A coffin was made for him in anticipation of his death, which he used as a wardrobe. The print above was possibly used as a fundraiser tool for him.

Fig. 38
A. R. Burt
John Evans
1819

Fig. 39
Dean Shaw
Toni Iommi,
Black Sabbath,
Donnington
2012

In 1965, the 17-year-old Anthony Frank – a budding guitarist – lost the tip of his middle finger and part of the ring finger of his right hand in an accident at a sheet metal factory in Birmingham. This injury affected his playing style and, as it turned out, popular music history. To ease the string tension on his injured hand he detuned his guitar – his bassist followed suit and they developed a foreboding minor-key sound that became a mainstay of heavy metal music. Anthony Frank is now known as Tony Iommi – lead guitarist and songwriter in Black Sabbath – his sacrificed fingers an offering to the machines, creating a new type of twentieth-century industrial music. His injury is not so different from those occurring 100 years before:

'Little boys and girls are here seen at work at the tip-punching machines (all acting by steam power) with their fingers in constant danger of being punched off once in every second, while at the same time they have their heads between whirling wheels a few inches distant from each ear. "They seldom lose the hand", said one of the proprietors to me, in explanation; "it only takes a finger at the first or second joint. Sheer carelessness – looking about them – sheer carelessness!' — Mr. Horne's Report, *Parliamentary Papers*, 1843, quoted in E. Royston Pike, *Human Documents of the Industrial Revolution in Britain*, 1970

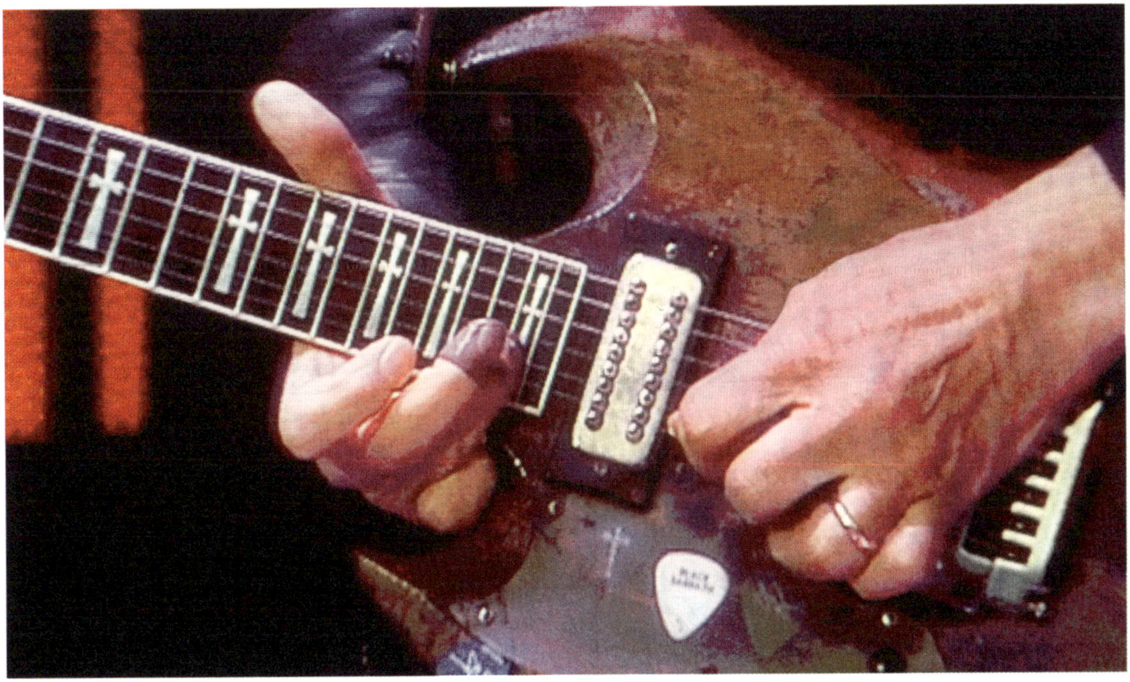

It was not unusual for factory accidents, or even the mundane incidents and experiences of nineteenth-century industrial life, to be recorded and memorialised in a type of popular song known as the 'broadside' – a musical form that gave a voice to the new working-class experience. Sold in the street, often in the absence of newspapers, the broadside was a truly reactive form of urban music.

The broadside offered up similar themes to the American blues music so beloved of Iommi and his peers: migration, exploitation, sex and the tough new world of work. 'The New Bury Loom' is a masterpiece of workplace erotica and innuendo, using the technical language of weaving to tell a story of love amongst the machines. It also speaks of the new relationship between worker and technology. There is love of a different kind in 'Utick's Trip to Manchester', a classic cautionary tale in which the protagonist travels from the countryside to the corrupt city, where he is taken in by a woman, only to later discover that she is a prostitute.

Though often comical, they also articulated the social and human stresses that the rapid rate of change in the industrial era had brought about. 'Jone O' Grinfield' a misery protest song about the plight of an impoverished cotton weaver, carries suggestions of insurrection if the workers' situation does not improve. The popularity of broadsides waned with the advent of the music hall, a more organised form of mass entertainment, in which songs became associated with specific performers, setting the trend for popular music as we know it.

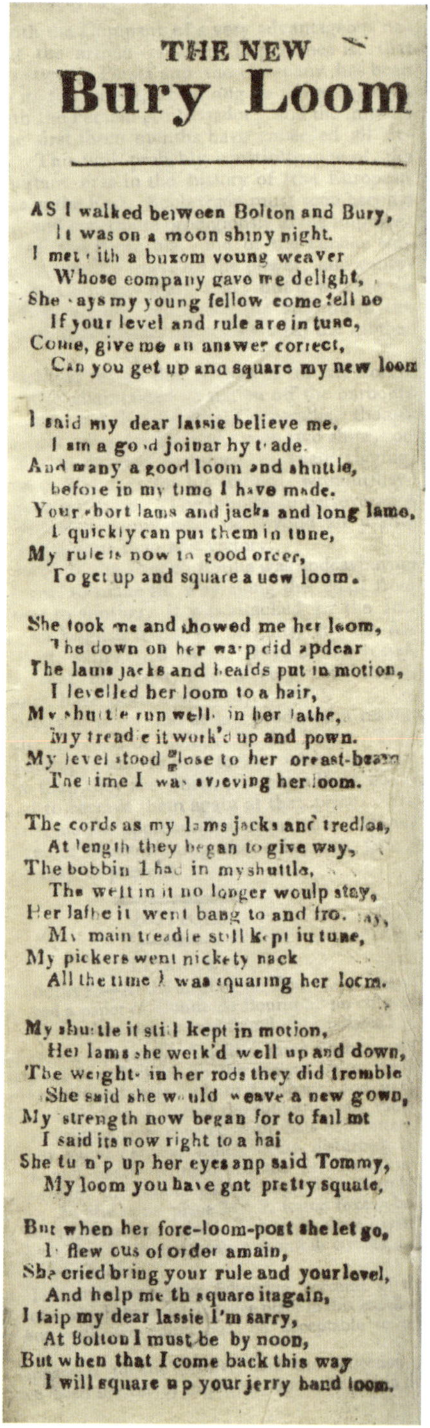

THE NEW
Bury Loom

AS I walked between Bolton and Bury,
It was on a moon shiny night.
I met with a buxom young weaver
Whose company gave me delight,
She says my young fellow come tell me
If your level and rule are in tune,
Come, give me an answer correct,
Can you get up and square my new loom

I said my dear lassie believe me,
I am a good joinar by trade.
And many a good loom and shuttle,
before in my time I have made.
Your short lams and jacks and long lamo,
I quickly can put them in tune,
My rule is now in good order,
To get up and square a new loom.

She took me and showed me her loom,
The down on her warp did appear
The lams jacks and healds put in motion,
I levelled her loom to a hair,
My shuttle run well in her lathe,
My treadle it work'd up and pown.
My level stood close to her breast-beam
The time I was weaving her loom.

The cords as my lams jacks and tredles,
At length they began to give way,
The bobbin I had in myshuttle,
The weft in it no longer woulp stay,
Her lathe it went bang to and fro.
My main treadle still kept in tune,
My pickers went nickety nack
All the time I was squaring her loom.

My shuttle it still kept in motion,
Her lams she work'd well up and down,
The weights in her rods they did tremble
She said she would weave a new gown,
My strength now began for to fail mt
I said its now right to a hai
She turn'p up her eyes anp said Tommy,
My loom you have got pretty squate,

But when her fore-loom-post she let go,
It flew out of order amain,
She cried bring your rule and your level,
And help me th square it again,
I saip my dear lassie I'm sarry,
At Bolton I must be by noon,
But when that I come back this way
I will square up your jerry band loom.

Fig. 40
'The New
Bury Loom'
Early nineteenth
century

Fig. 41
'Utick's Trip
to Manchester'
Early nineteenth
century

UTICK'S TRIP TO
MANCHESTER.

Come listen to my story, a lesson you may learn,
aud by my advice your good wishes I would earn
You wild and rakish young men who often go astra
By tripping down to Manchester upou a Whit-Sunday,
Fal di dal di dido, fal di dal di day.

'Tis of a bonny Utick fro' Millbottom side,
Who took a trip to Manchester upon a Whitsuntide,
If that were all about it there's noihing wrong in that,
But he stabled his pony at the sign of Dog aud Rat.

A pretty little damsel she sat upou his knee,
She said my bonny Utick come fly away with me,
There is a cozy back slum a little to the right,
And if you have any money we will nestle there to-night

Says Utick I have money, besides a little wit,
Thou wants to share it I know, but that will never fit,
You think that I'm a lumyed, a joskin and a clown,
And you'll send me back to Oldham withou a single brown.

Says Utick I remember my pall Jammy Poss,
A fose un were he, but you pooden him across,
Un Jammy awlus tells me, a mon with any seuse,
Would never go to Manchester with more nor eighteen-pence.

To think uv Brass Dan is a caution I declare,
For o' he had a fortune you geet'n th' best share,
Egad you geet it o' for you didna leaAe a meg,
Un you turnthim on to wide-world to starve or else to beg

Says the damsel I would not have done such a thiug,
And she huddled and she cuddled under Utick's wing,
She hoaxed aud she coaxed till he gave his consent,
Then arm in arm together down Deansgate they weAt

Now Utick was as merry as a bird could be,
And he sang like a thrush in a gooseberry tree,
But he changed his tune ere the dawning of the more,
For he cursed the day and the hour he was born.

He shivered and he shook at the corner of a street,
He had moulted his feathers and wur lapt in a sheet,
He'd lost his brass, and what made it wur,
They dropt him in a back slum through a e,ap dur.

A bobby coming bye and shining his lamp,
He thought it wur a ghost, and began to decamp,
But Utick he shouted, and shouted amain,
If you send me back to Owdham awl never coma again.

'Twur somehow or other aw conna tell how,
He geet to th' Millbothom and he's still there now,
He wur ill a bit ut afther, but now he's o reet,
For Dr. Larry's pills have set him on his feet.

ACT ON
THE SQUARE

Thro' being fond of acting right,
Straightforward, Just aud Fair,
I try to make my troubles light,
And little do I care.
As happy as a king I live,
On just what I can spare,
And from experience I give
This hint—act on the square.

CHORUS.

Act on the square boys, act on the square,
Upright and fair boys, act oa the square
Act on the square boys, act on the square,
Upright and fair boys, act on the square.

Nw in the streets a thing so bad.
Which often is the case,
A swellish, foolish-looking lad,
Some modest girl will chaset,
Then square you round and let him see
If he annoyance dare;
You'll give him striking proofs
How to act on the square.

When out one night with noisy swells
The Haymarket kept alive,
One Sergeant *W.* with oyster shells,
To pelt they did contrive;
They nearly get into disgrace,
But squaring served them there,
And brightly shone the bobby's face,
Who liked to see things square.

I never liked a round game, nay
Round tables I can't abear,
And in a Circus I can't stay,
So I live in a Square,
Now brothers all, and Masons too,
Of good lets do ou share,
And when a chance does present itself
We must act on the square.

Fig. 42
'Jone O'Grinfield'
c. 1860

Migration to cities, as touched upon in 'Utick's Trip to Manchester', was only enhanced by a dramatic population increase in the UK – from 8.9 million in 1801 to 13.9 million in just 30 years. Urbanisation separated the worker from traditional poor-relief arrangements, structured around the country parish. Cotton workers were at the sharp end of this change, entering into an industry of the new factory owners' invention, where poor pay meant that whole families were forced to work in cotton mills. Handloom-weaver pay decreased from 23s per week in 1805 to 6s 3d in 1833, as mechanisation took away the need for skilled labour. Income suppression was used, in turn, as a form of social control: subsistence wages ensured worker obedience and willingness to work. These days, high rent has a similar effect, whilst depressing domestic demand and taking an increasing percentage of income. All the while the new middle classes were creating an increasingly unequal society, as this description of Manchester illustrates:

'There is no town in the world where the distance between the rich and the poor is so great or the barrier between them so difficult to be crossed... There is far less personal communication between the master cotton spinner and his workmen, between the calico printer and his blue-handed boys, between the master tailor and his apprentices, than there is between the Duke of Wellington and the humblest labourer on his estate.' — Canon Parkinson, *On the Present Condition of the Labouring Poor in Manchester*, 1841

These class divisions in the workplace persisted beyond the Industrial Revolution and became a feature of the steady post-war decline of UK industry. Labour was becoming an abstracted element in the economic process, at the very time when unprecedented pressure was being placed upon the mass of people working in cities. The belief in the importance of a supportive society was losing currency among the emerging managing class. Thomas Carlyle identified this obsession with a mechanistic interpretation of human relationships:

'Not the external and physical alone is now managed by machinery but the internal and spiritual also... The same habit regulates not our modes of action alone, but our modes of thought and feeling. Men are grown mechanical in head and heart, as well as in hand. They have lost faith in individual endeavours, and in natural force, or any kind. Not for internal perfection, but for external combinations and arrangements for institutions, constitutions, for mechanism of one sort or another, do they hope and struggle.' —Thomas Carlyle, *Signs of the Times*, 1829

JONE O'GRINFIELD.

I'm a poor cotton weaver as many one knows,
I've nowt to eat i'th house an I've worn out my cloas,
You'd hardly give sixpence for all I have on,
My clugs they are brossen and stockings I've none,
You'd think it wur hard to be sent into th' world,
To clem and do th' best ot you con.

Our church parson kept telling us long,
We should have better times if we'd hold our tongues,
I've houden my tongue till I can hardly draw breath,
I think i' my heart he means to clem me to death;
I know he lives weel by backbiting the de'il,,
But he he never pickced o'er in his life.

I tarried six week an thought every day wur t' last,
I tarried and shifted till now I'm quite fast;
I lived on nettles while nettles were good,
An Waterloo porridge were best of my food;
I'm telling you true I can find folks enew,
That are living no better than me.

Old Bill o' Dan's sent bailiffs one day,
For a shop score I owed him that I could not pay,
But he wur too late for old Bill o' Bent,
Had sent tit and cart and taen goods for rent,
We had nou bur a stoo, that wur a seat for two,
And on it cowered Margit and me.

The bailiffs looked round assly as a mouse,
When they saw aw things were taen out ot house,
Says one to the other all's gone thou may see,
Aw sed lads never fret you're welcome to me;
They made no more ado, but nipp'd up th' owd stoo,
And we both went wack upoth flags.

I geet howd of Margit for hoo wur strucken sick,
Hoo sed hoo ne'er had such a bang sin hoo wur wick
The bailiffs scoured off with owd stoo on their backs,
They would not have cared had they brook our necks,
They're mad at owd Bent cos he's taen goods for rent,
And wur ready to flee us alive.

I sed to our Margit as we lay upoth floor,
We shall never be lower in this world I'm sure,
But if we alter I'm sure we mun mend ,
For I think in my heart we are both at far end,
For meat we have none nor looms to weave on,
Egad they're as weel lost as found.

Then I geet up my piece and I took it em back
I scarcely dare speak mester looked so black,
He said you wur o'erpaid last time you coom,
I said if I wur 'twas for weaving bout loom;
In a mind as I'm in I'll ne'er pick o'er again,
For I've woven mysel toth' fur end.

Then aw coom out and left him to chew that,
When aw thought again aw wur vext till aw sweat,
To think that we mun work to keep them and awth set,
All the day o' my life and still be in their debt;
So I'll give o'er trade an work with a spade,
Or go and break stones upoth road,

Our Margit declared if hoo'd cloas to put on,
Hoo'd go up to Lundun an see the big mon
An if things didn't alter when hoo had been,
Hoo swears hoo'd feight blood up toth e'en,
Hoo's nought again th' Queen but likes a fair thing,
An hoo says hoo can tell when hoo's hurt.

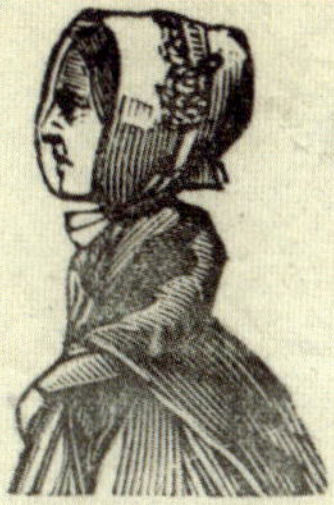

SALLY SLY.

Printed and Sold Wholesale and Retail, by
[illegible]gton [illegible]den-street, Oldham
Road, Manchester.

At six in the morning awaking,
Coals taking,
Love making,
With barrow, I cry;
I knock and sing at the areas,
My care is
The fairies,
With coals to supply.

I'm in love! I'm in love! Oh my eye!
I'm going for to meet her to-morrow—
Sally Sly! Sally Sly! Sally Sly!
I'm going for to meet her to-morrow—
Sally Sly! Sally Sly! Sally Sly!

We meet where the walls they've been (chalking,
While walking
And talking;
We're both tall and straight,
With apples and cherries I treat her
Sweet creature,
I meet her
To-morrow, at eight.
I'm in love, &c.

One day, Jemmy Raspell, the baker,
To take her
And make her
His tool, he did try;
He told her to kick Jemmy Snivel
To the devil—
How civil;
Then she blacken'd his eye.
I'm in love, &c.

32.

Fig. 43
Thomas Alm
Swainson Birley Cotton Mill, Near Preston, Lancashire
1834

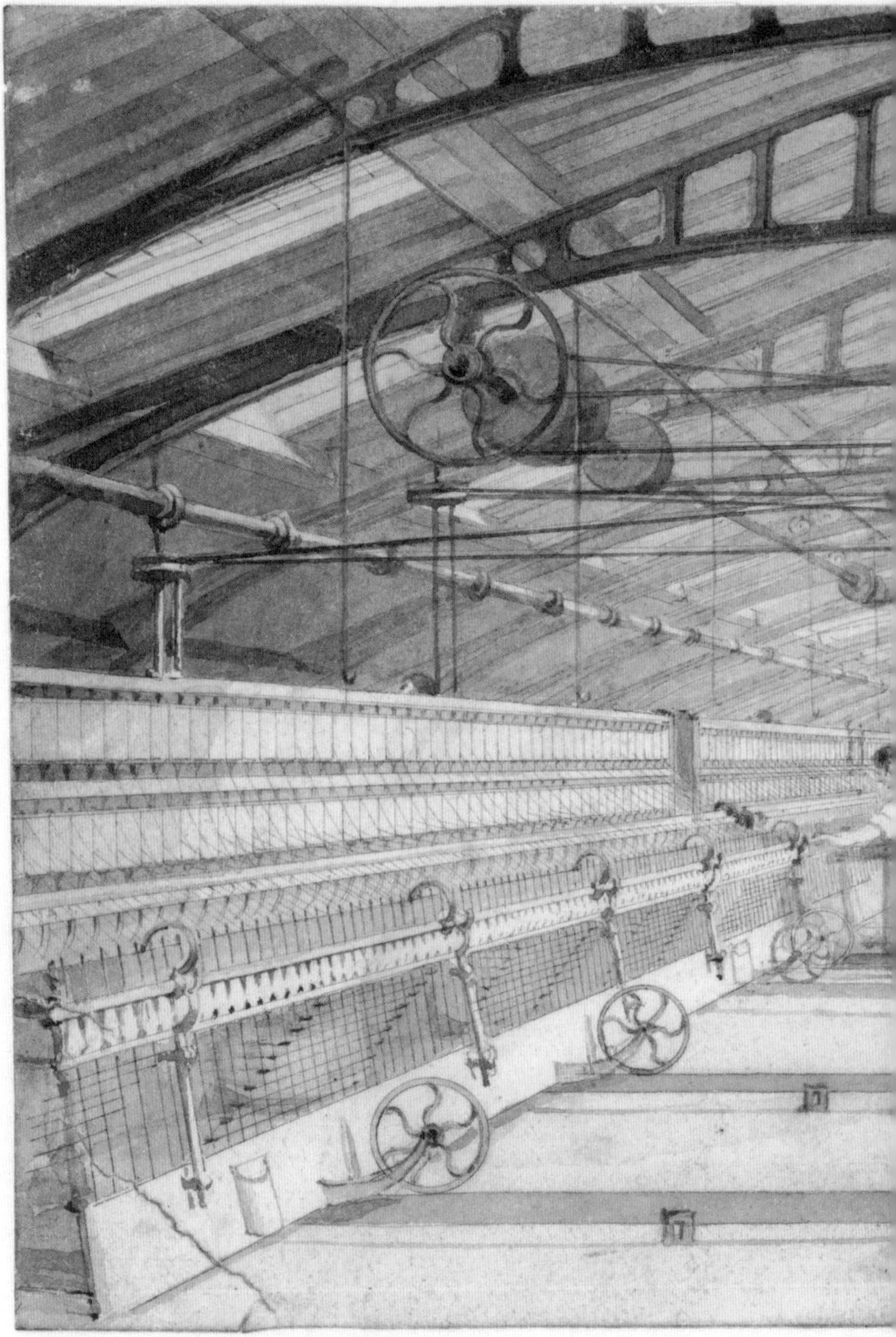

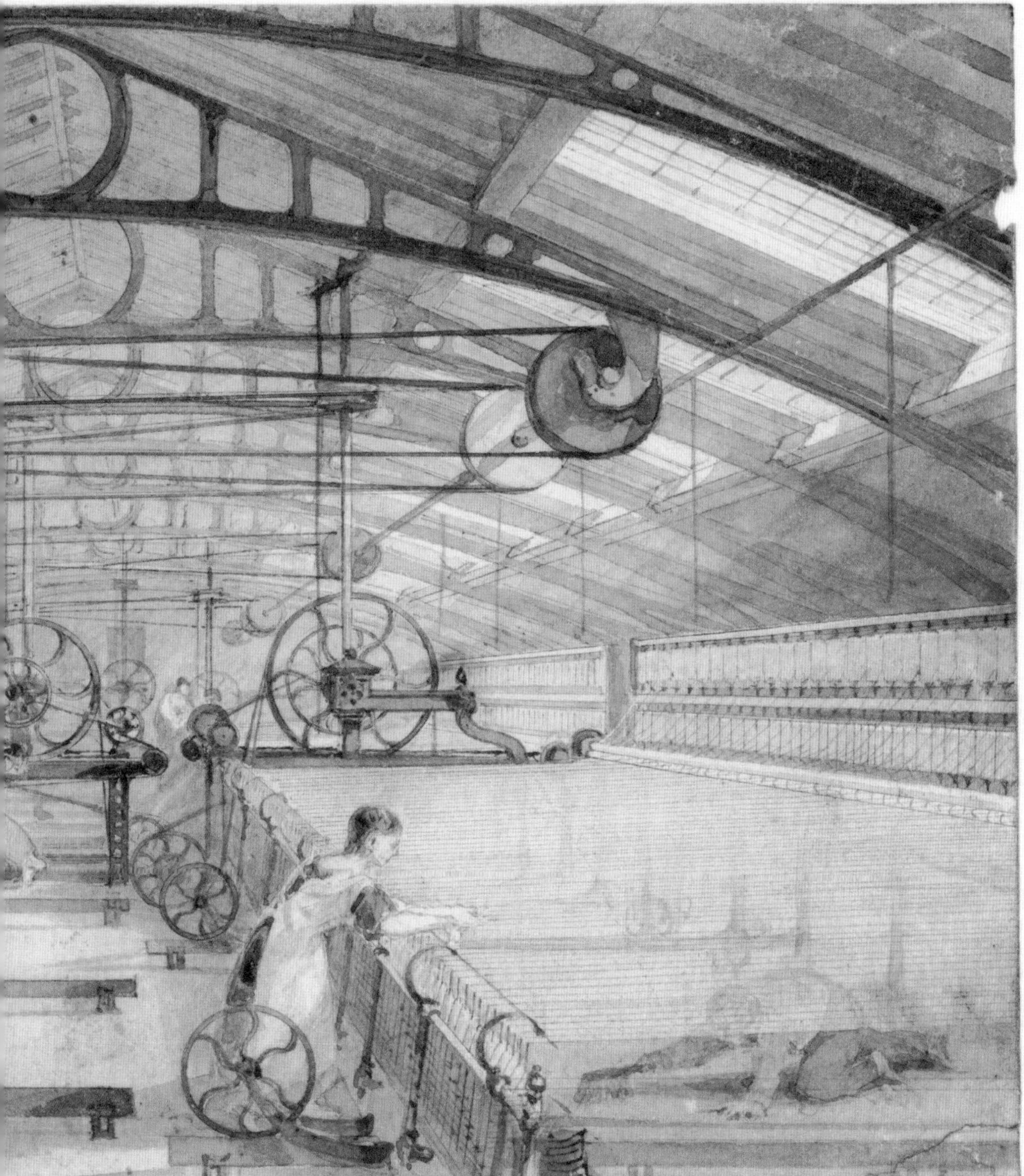

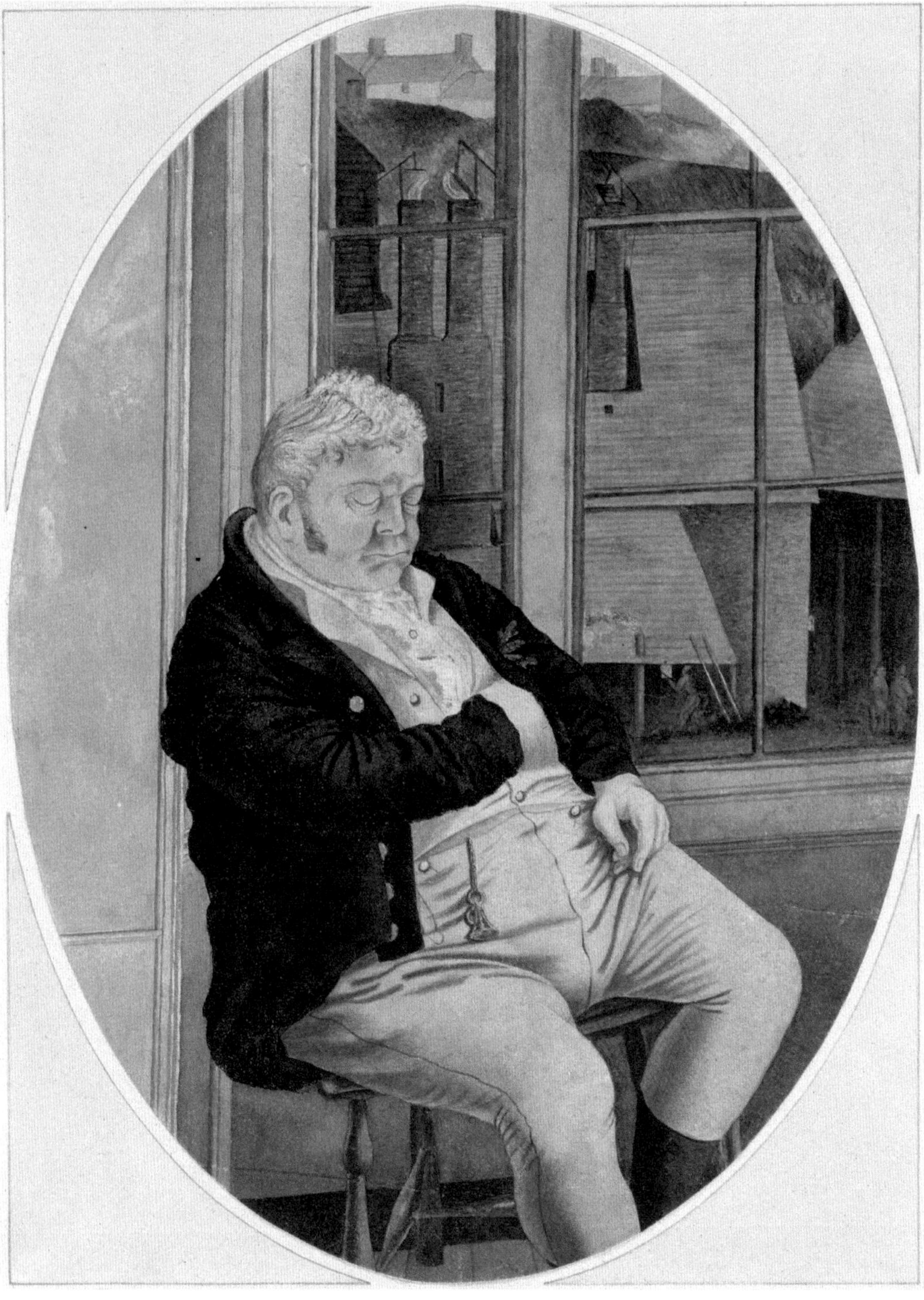

Fig. 44
John Petherick
Ironworks Manager Dozing
c. 1830

Fig. 45
Robert Havell
Factory Children
1814

This inevitably led to abuses, especially of the young – the lowest of the low in the production process.

'Alexander Dean, overlooker in a flax-mill at Dundee… having no parents to take care of him, he obtained his first job at the age of 12 in a flax mill in Dundee, where they worked no less than 17 hours a day, exclusive of meals, and for wages "sometimes we got the clothes which were taken from others who deserted the service". Was beaten very often. His story continued: "One time I was struck by the master on the head with his clenched fist, and kicked, when I was down. I saw one girl trailed by the hair of her head, and kicked by him, when she was down, till she roared 'Murder!' several times. The girl told me that the master had wished to use familiarities with her, and she had refused the night before; and he found a small deficiency in her work, and he took the opportunity of abusing her."' — 'The Girl Who Got Away', cited in E. Royston Pike, *Human Documents of the Industrial Revolution in Britain*, 1970

This account is taken from the 1832 parliamentary report into the employment of children in factories. Even those in the middle classes who believed in the self-regulating nature of the factory system realised that their livelihoods were threatened if social meltdown did occur. There was an increasing awareness that this fast-moving social and technological change was unsustainable, as people took stock of what had been happening underground and in factory buildings in the preceding 40 years. It's not too far fetched to compare this situation to today, as we begin to fully understand how the digital revolution has changed the world and our relationship to the world.

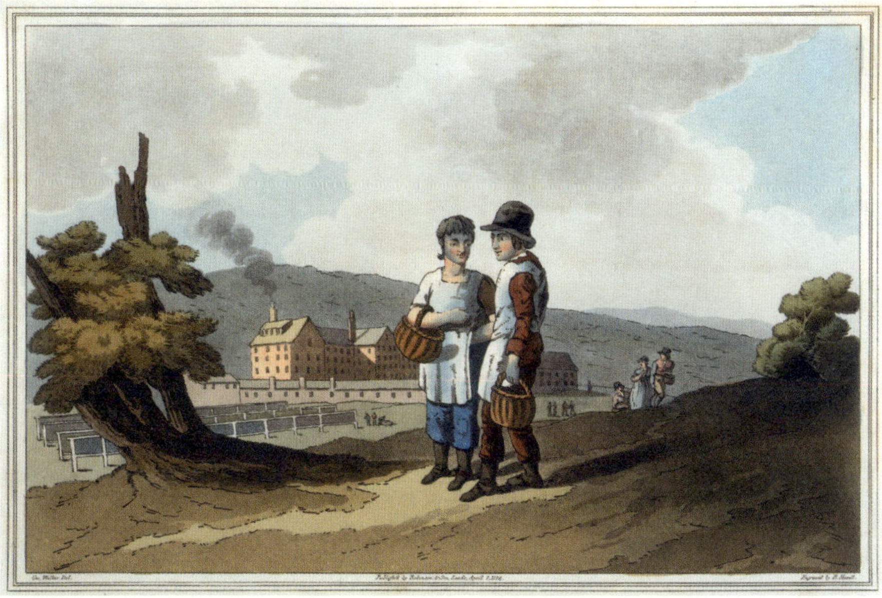

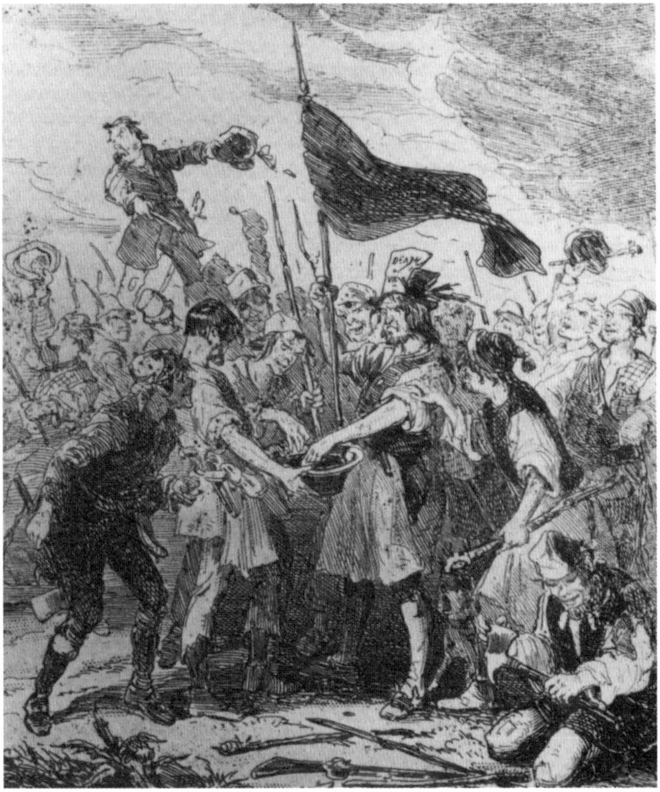

In the new industrial cities, the unprecedented concentration of people and, more importantly, ideas could and did lead to unrest to the point that whole towns were occupied by workers. By the middle of the decade known as the 'hungry forties', Friedrich Engels noted that, 'in this country social war is under full headway' (*The Condition of the Working Class in England*, 1845). The Merthyr Rising of 1831, in South Wales, is thought to have been the first occasion that the red flag was raised in protest. The anger and imagery used in descriptions of the event are primal – at odds with portraits of local workers only a few years later. And it's easy to see how the events scared the life out of the authorities.

'At Hirwaun, up on Aberdare Mountain, the rebels ritually sacrificed a calf, washed a flag in its blood and impaled a loaf of bread on the staff. His arms drenched to the elbows, the bearer set off with his bloody talisman of the people's martial law to summon the 'Sons of Vulcan' to insurrection.'
— Gwyn A. Williams, introduction to John Gorman, *Banner Bright*, 1973

The portraits of the workers from Hirwaun and Treforest are distinctly at odds with the revolutionary temper of the times in South Wales. The paintings were produced when Francis Crawshay was running the factories. Crawshay ran an unorthodox business, living with one of the workers and siring children with a number of others. The fact that we still know all the names of those painted is notable, when compared to the anonymity of the women steelworkers.

Fig. 46
Merthyr Rising
1831

Fig. 47
W. J. Chapman
Francis Crawshay Workers Portraits
1835
(and overleaf)

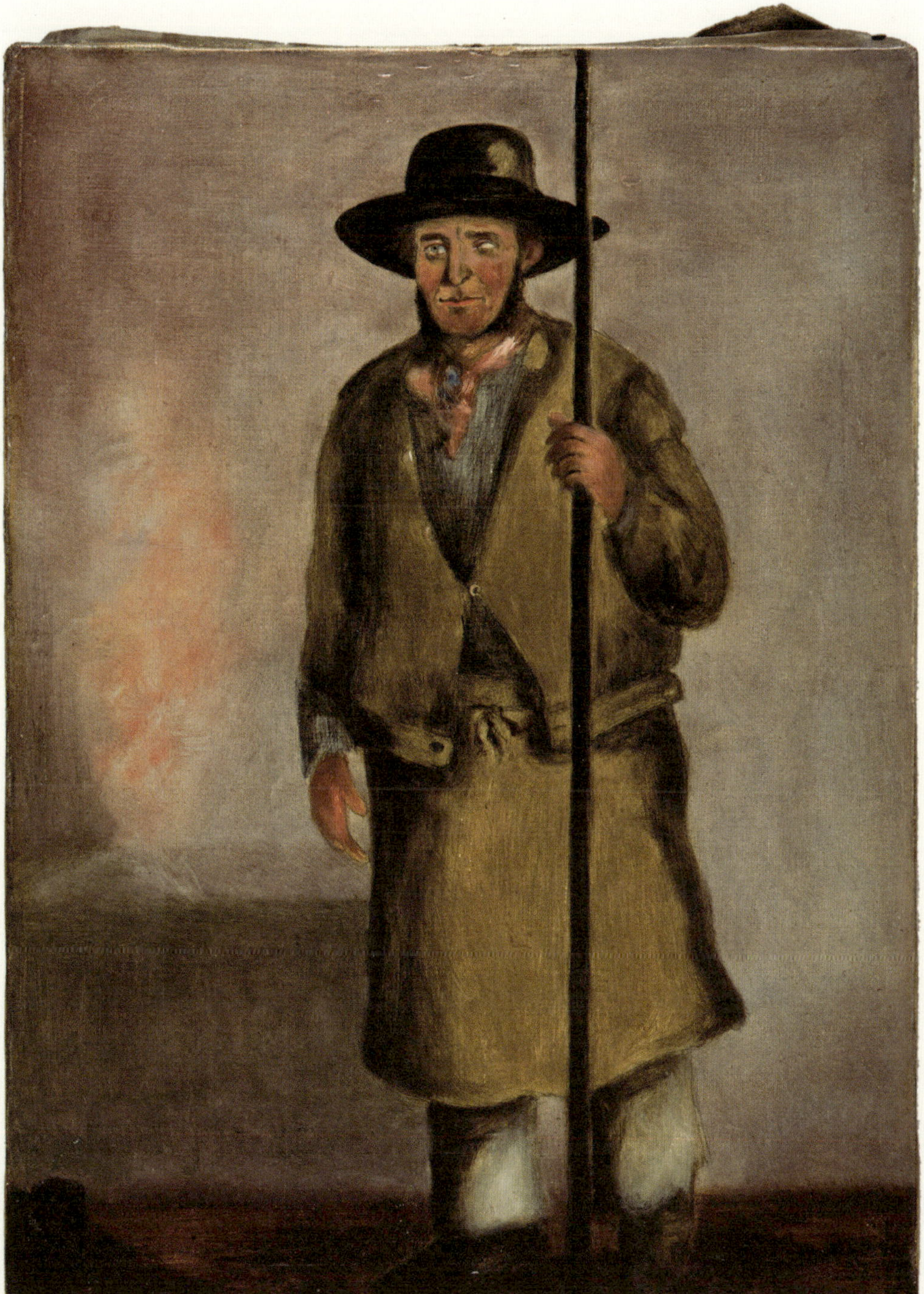

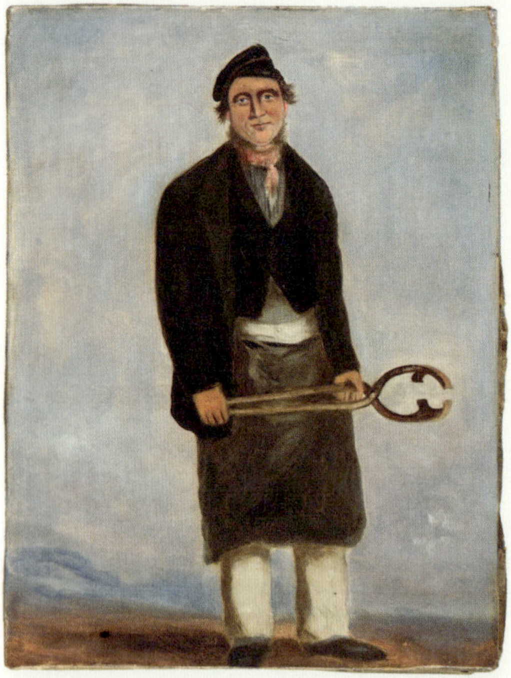
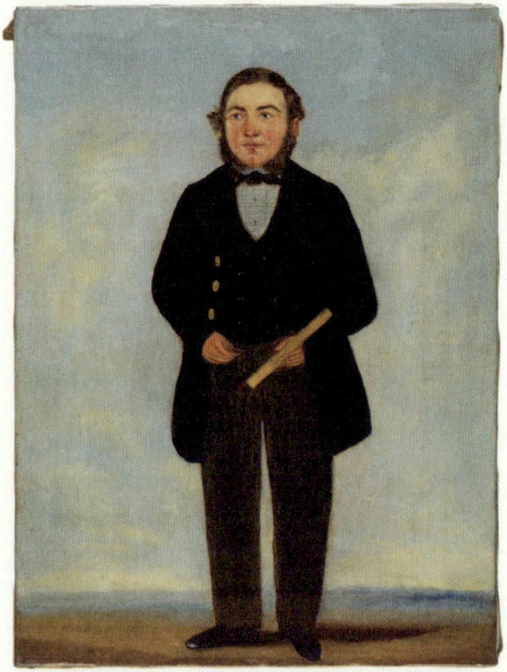
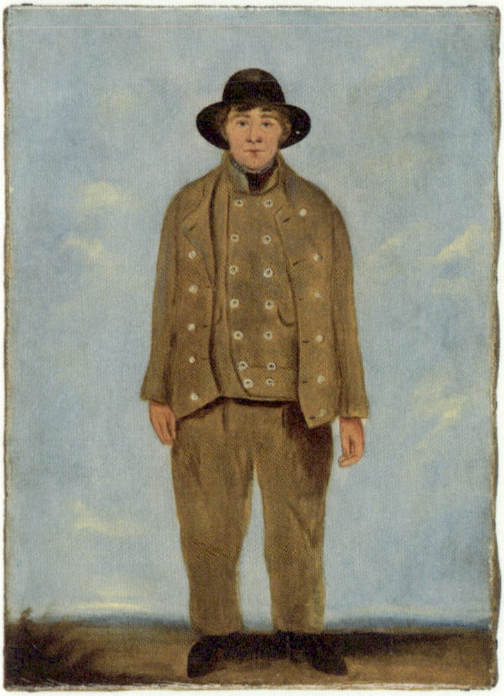
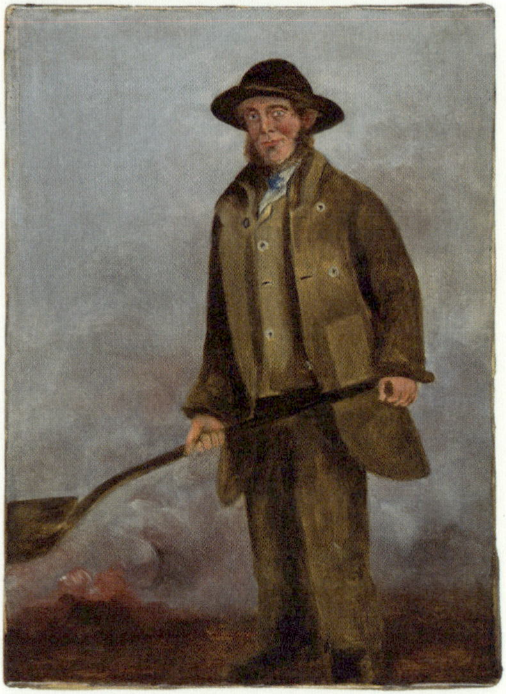

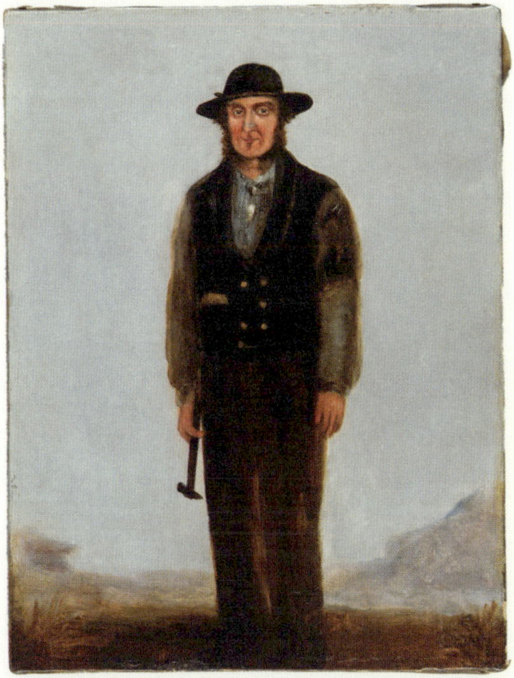

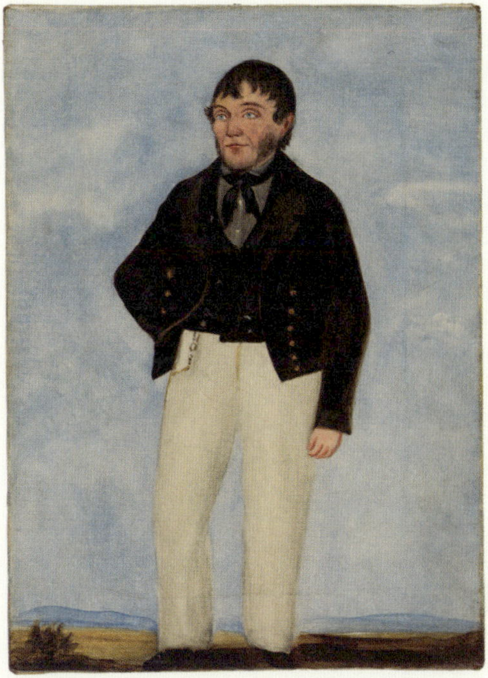

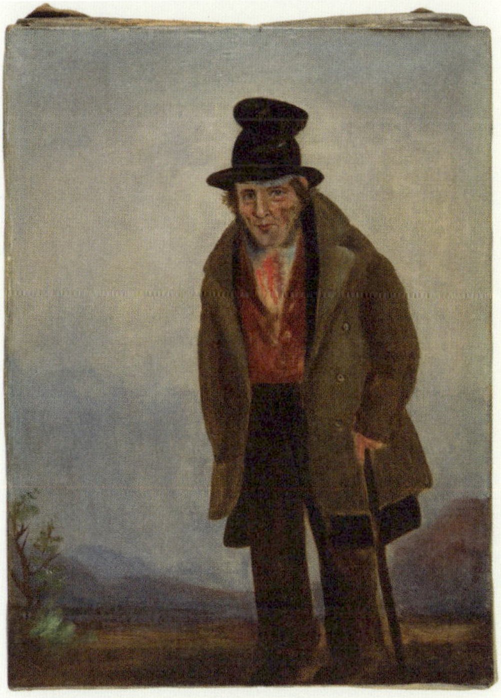

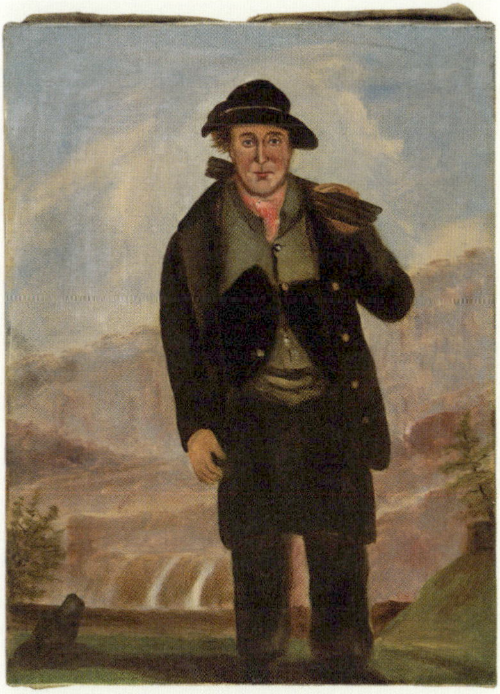

Strikes and protests were often incorrectly defined by their criminality rather than the political or social grievances they were trying to address. A contemporary concern about street crime confused the issue, with fears around gangs almost quaint in comparison to the impending threat of social meltdown.

The street gang is a uniquely urban phenomenon – concerned with defence of an area, street, or corner even – of which the 'scuttlers' were a late-Victorian example. These young men were identified by their elaborate hairstyles and colourful scarves – a precursor to and influence on the 'teddy boys' of the next century, unlikely embodiments of Hobsbawm's description of the city dweller, who 'no longer need[s] tradition, they [are] their own reward' (Eric Hobsbawm, *Labouring Men*, 1964).

Fig. 48
William Bramian, 'The Captain', Labourer, 20 Years
c. 1884

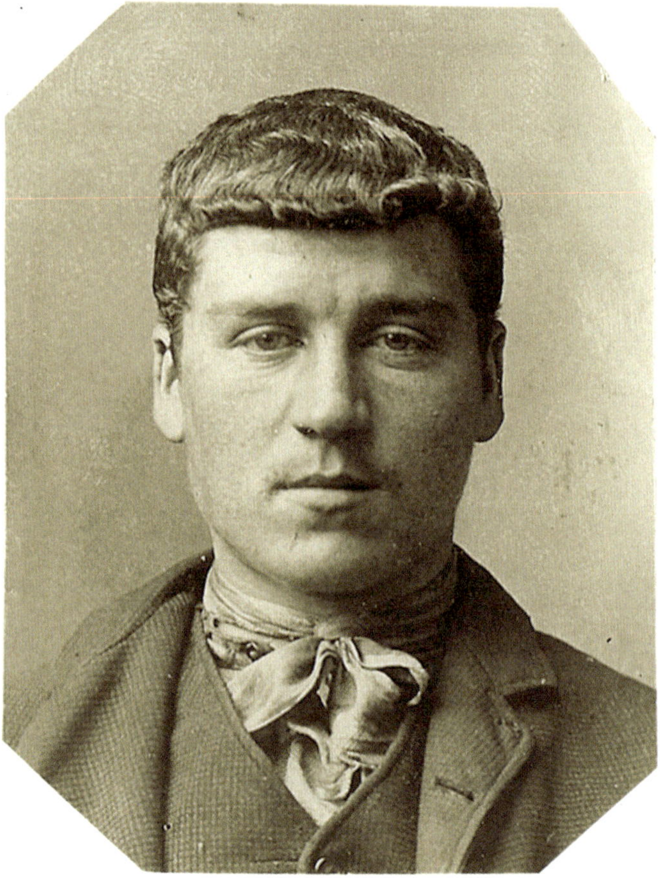

Fig. 49
(top left)
John Wallace,
Labourer, 18 Years
c. 1884

Fig. 50
(top right)
Patrick Hefferon,
Labourer, 20 Years
c. 1884

Fig. 51
(bottom left)
James Kerrighan,
Labourer, 19 Years
c. 1884

Fig. 52
(bottom right)
William Brooks,
Labourer, 20 Years
c. 1884

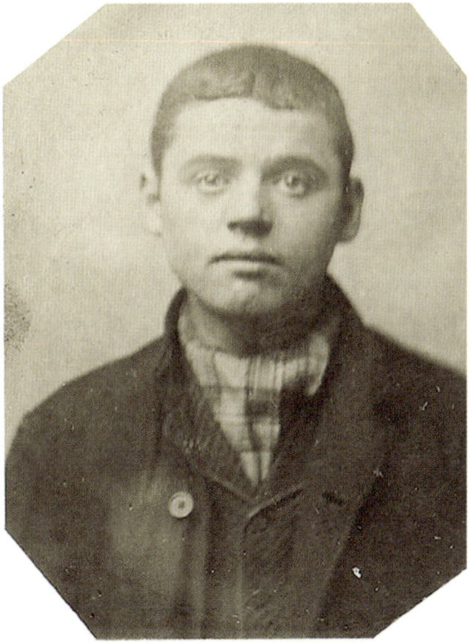

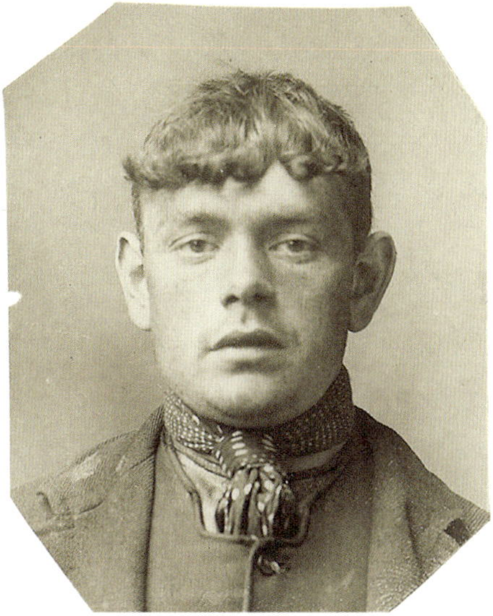

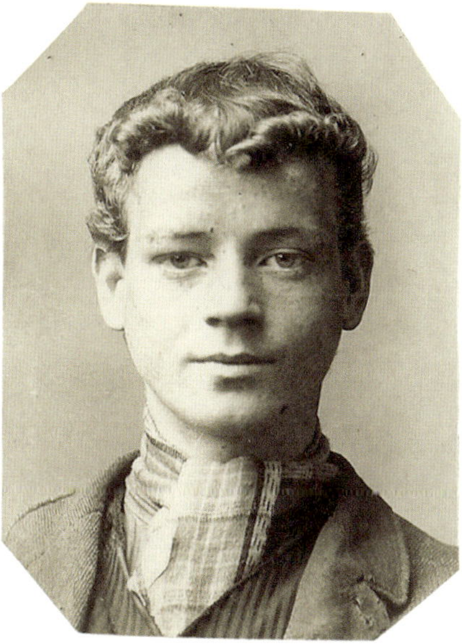

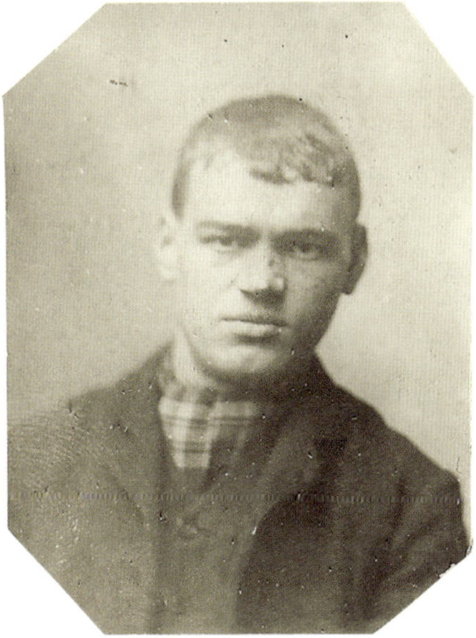

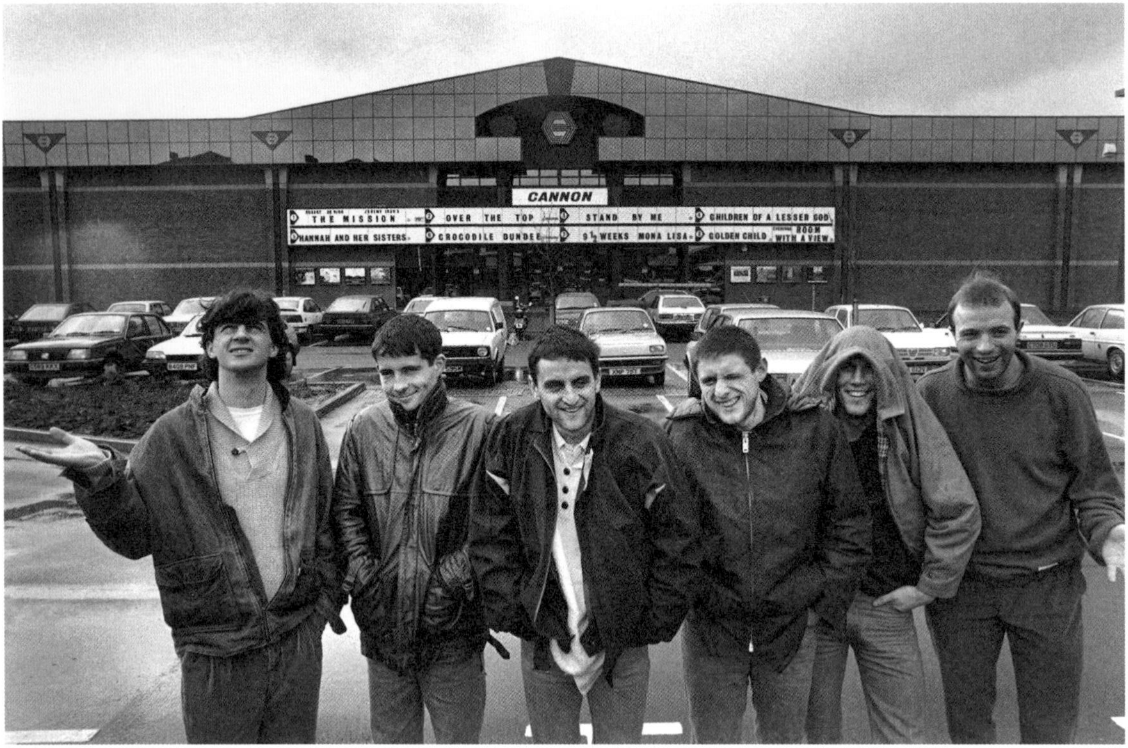

Not all gangs are united by criminality, most share common interests in sport or culture, and so the concept of the 'group' shares a direct lineage with the street gang. Furthermore, the cultivation of the blank stare to camera is more of a mug shot than a portrait – the uniform group identity and camaraderie are very similar. To be in a group is to be in an arrested state of adolescence, with licence to behave like a 16-year-old for the rest of your life.

Occasionally, though, echoes of the Industrial Revolution return through bands. In 1987, Ian Tilton and the Happy Mondays went on a tour of pre-Media City, Salford, to make some publicity shots. Though not quite as dramatic as the image of Adrian street and his father, these still show a group in a former industrial town that is trying to work out out what to do next. Shaun Ryder, the band's singer and songwriter, has a family tree that is a history lesson in itself.

Fig. 53
Ian Tilton
Happy Mondays, Salford
1987

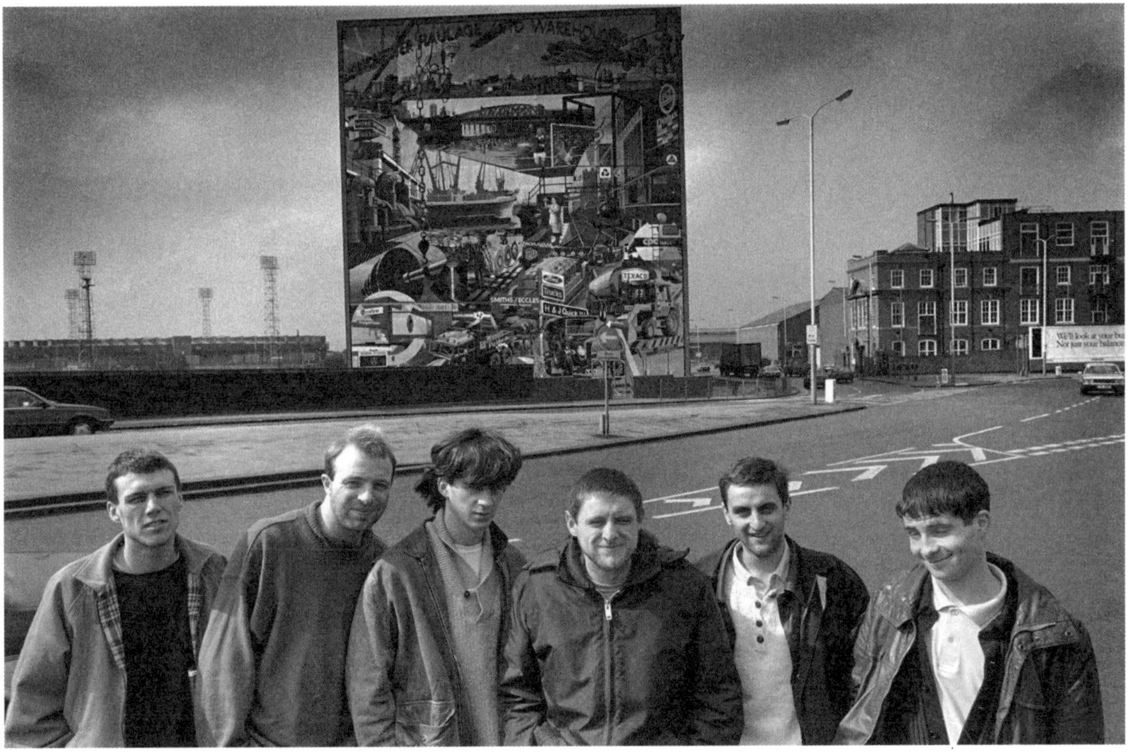

Fig. 54
Ian Tilton
Happy Mondays, Salford
1987

Fig. 55
Ian Tilton
Happy Mondays, Salford
1987

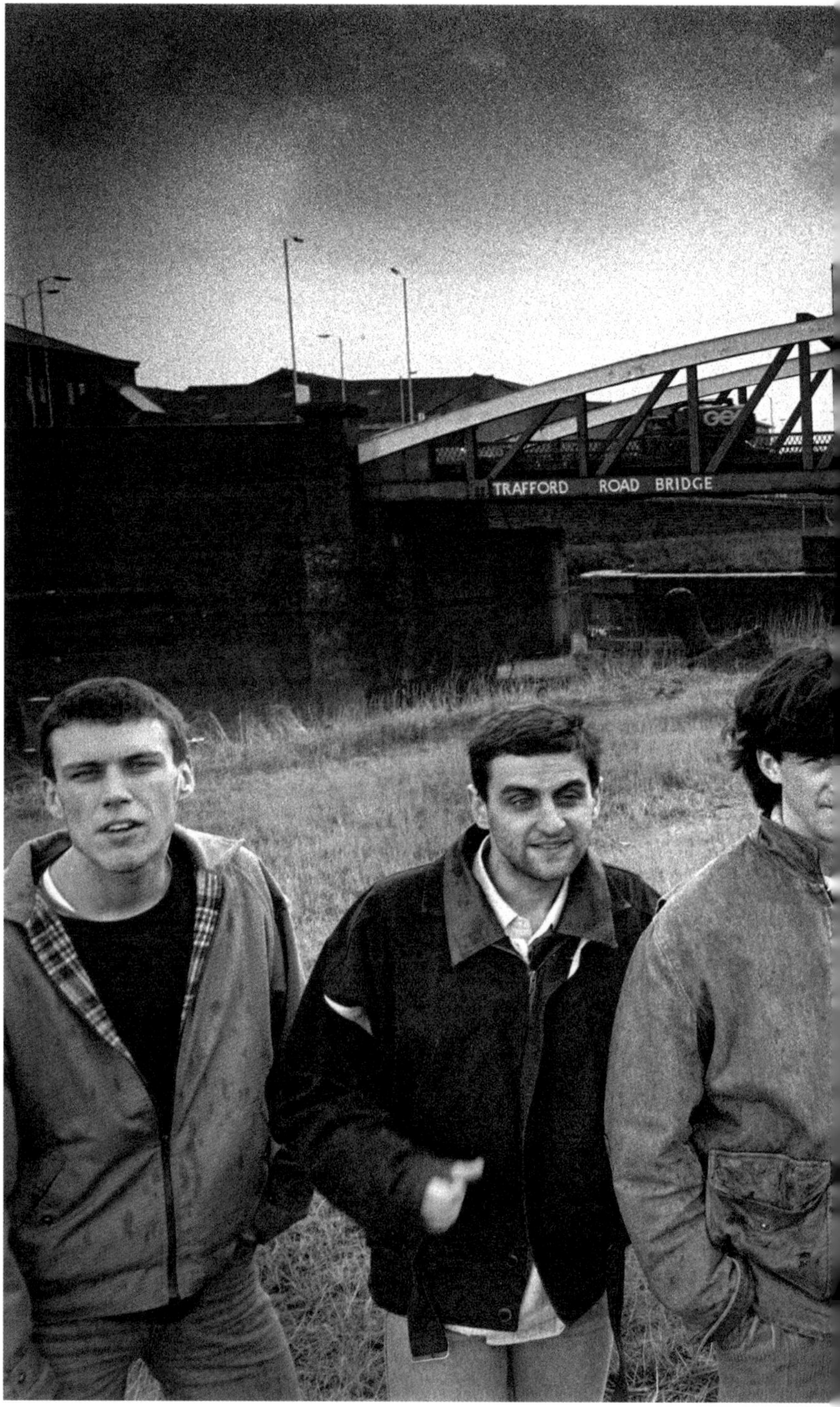

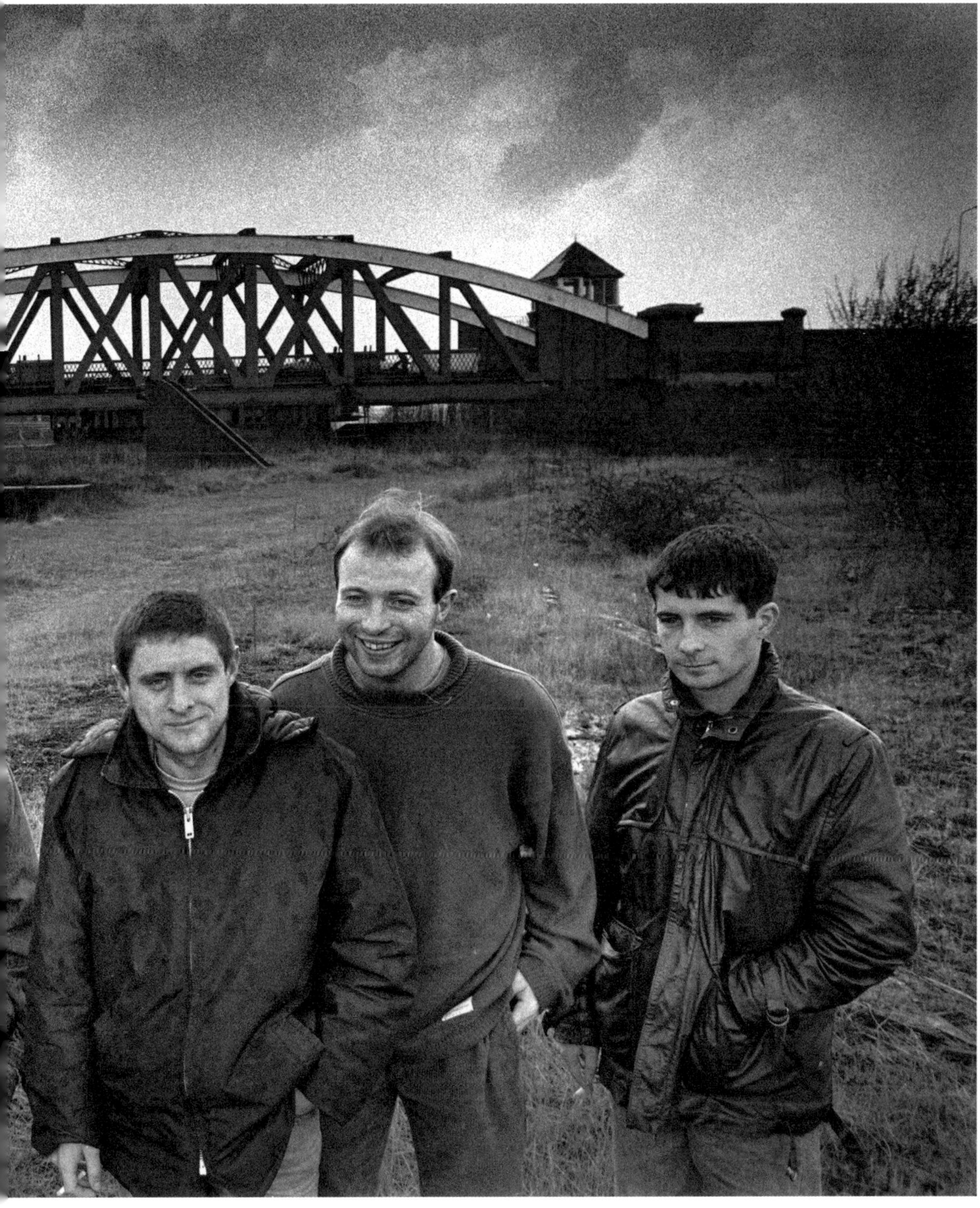

Richard Ryder
Born: 1830, Farnworth
Occupation: Millwright

Mary
Born: 1834, Wrightington

Joesph Greenhalgh
Born: 1835, Little Lever
Occupation: Coal miner

Elizabeth
Born: 1840, Prescott

John Fletcher

William Fletcher
Born: 1858, Derbyshire
Occupation: Labourer

James Baxendale
Born: 1823, Sapden
Occupation: Paper hanger

Jane Baxendale
Born: 1853, Salford

Helena
Born: 1822, Sapden

Edwin Ryder
Born: 1854, Wrightington
Occupation: Labourer

Hannah Ryder
Born: 1856, Farnworth
Occupation: Cotton weaver

William Arthur Ryder
Born: 1866, Farnworth
Occupation: Railway inspector/
Train shunter

Ann Greenhalgh
Born: 1859, Little Lever
Occupation: Cotton weaver

Mary Greenhalgh
Born: 1862, Little Lever
Occupation: Cotton weaver

Elizabeth Alice Greenhalgh
Born: 1868, Little Lever
Occupation: Cotton weaver

Susannah Greenhalgh
Born: 1875, Little Lever
Occupation: Cotton weaver

Peter Greenhalgh
Born: 1876, Little Lever
Occupation: Cloggers apprentice

Frederick Ryder
Born: 1913, Bolton
Occupation: Aircraft fitter/
Cotton operative

Emma Taylor
Workhouse orphan/illegitimate

Derek Ryder
Born: 1 November 1942, Farnworth
Occupation: Aircraft fitter/Roadie

Shaun William Ryder
Born: 23 August 1962, Little Hulton
Occupation: Singer

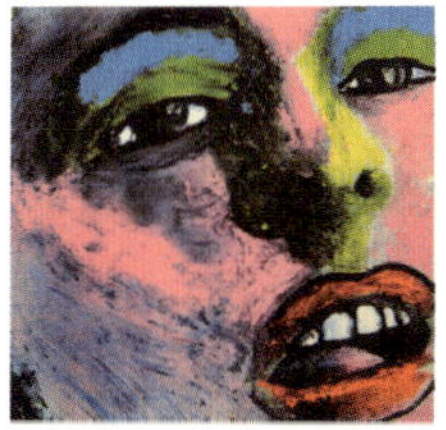

John Carroll
Occupation: Copper tube drawer

William Carroll
Born: 30 November 1919, Bolton
Occupation: Printer's assistant/
Copper tube drawer

Annie Linda Carroll
Born: 17 February 1942, Salford
Occupation: Housewife

Elizabeth Fletcher
Born: 1881
Occupation: Printing machine feeder

James Fletcher
Born: 1885
Occupation: Cloth stiffener

Jacob Fletcher
Born: 1891
Occupation: Cloth finisher

Mary Agnes Eastwood

Annie Fletcher
Born: 1920, Salford
Occupation: Staff nurse/
Copper tube drawer

Fig. 56
Jeremy Deller
Hallelujah!
Shaun Ryder's
Family Tree
2008

Fig. 57
John Davies
Stockport Viaduct
1986

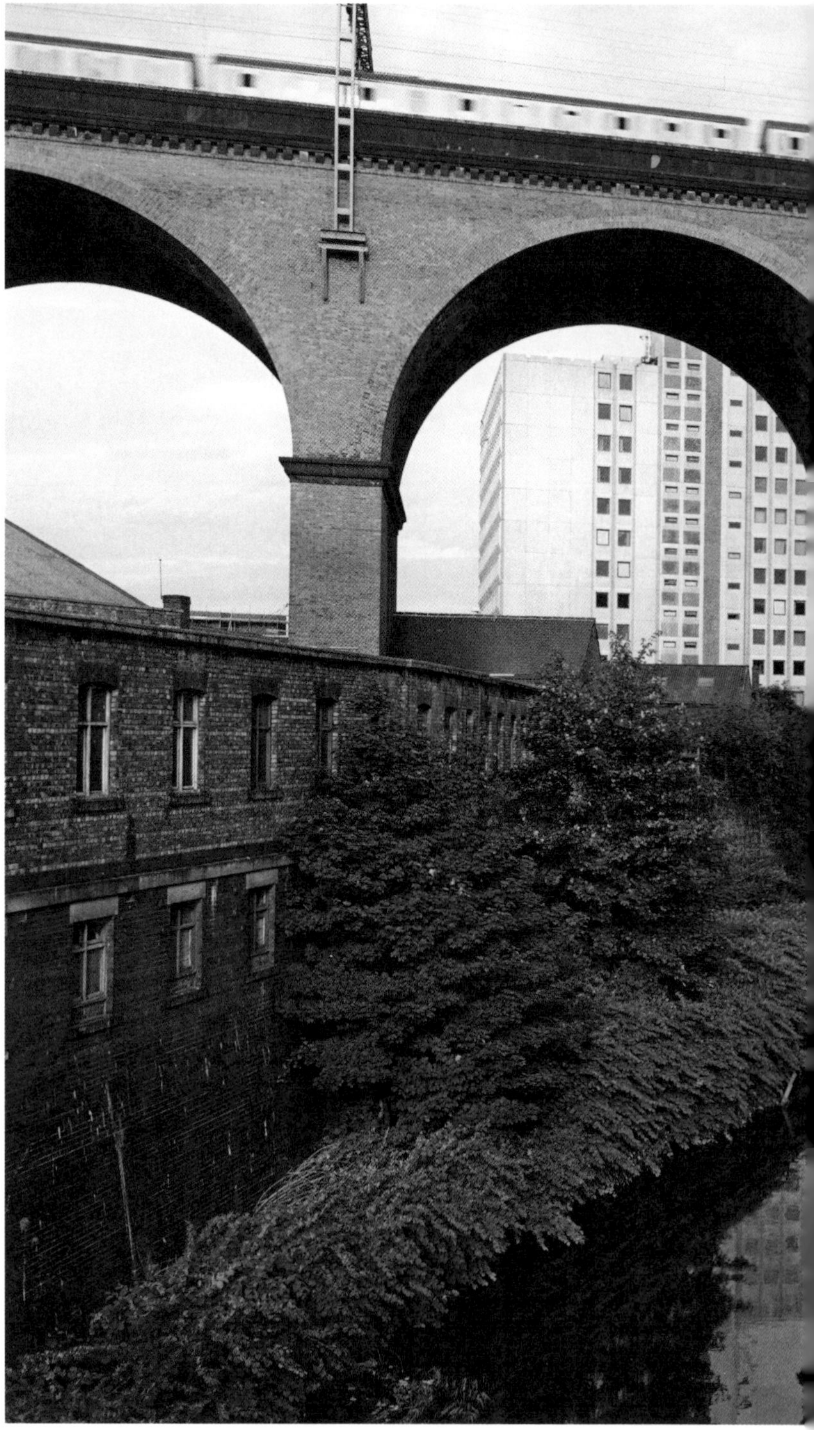

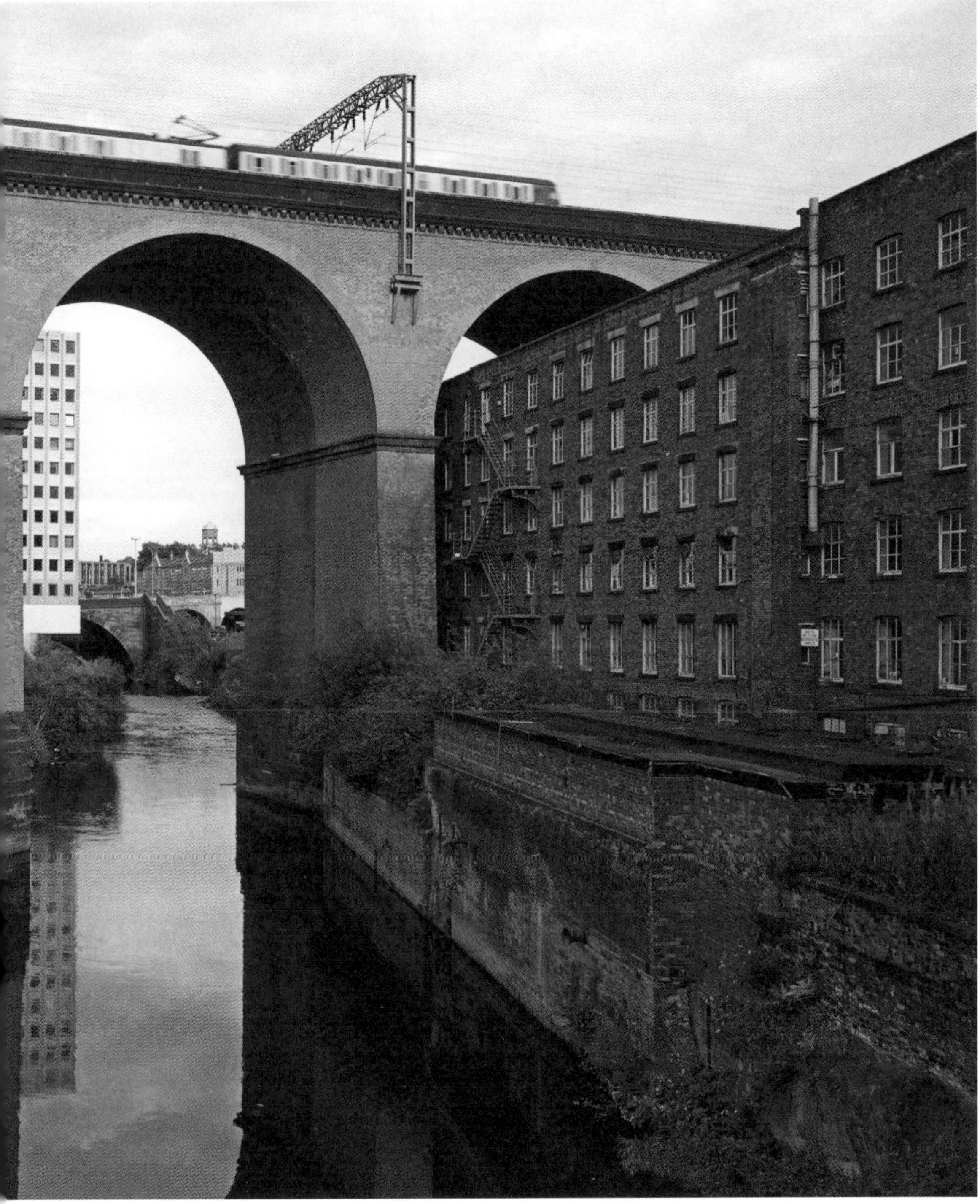

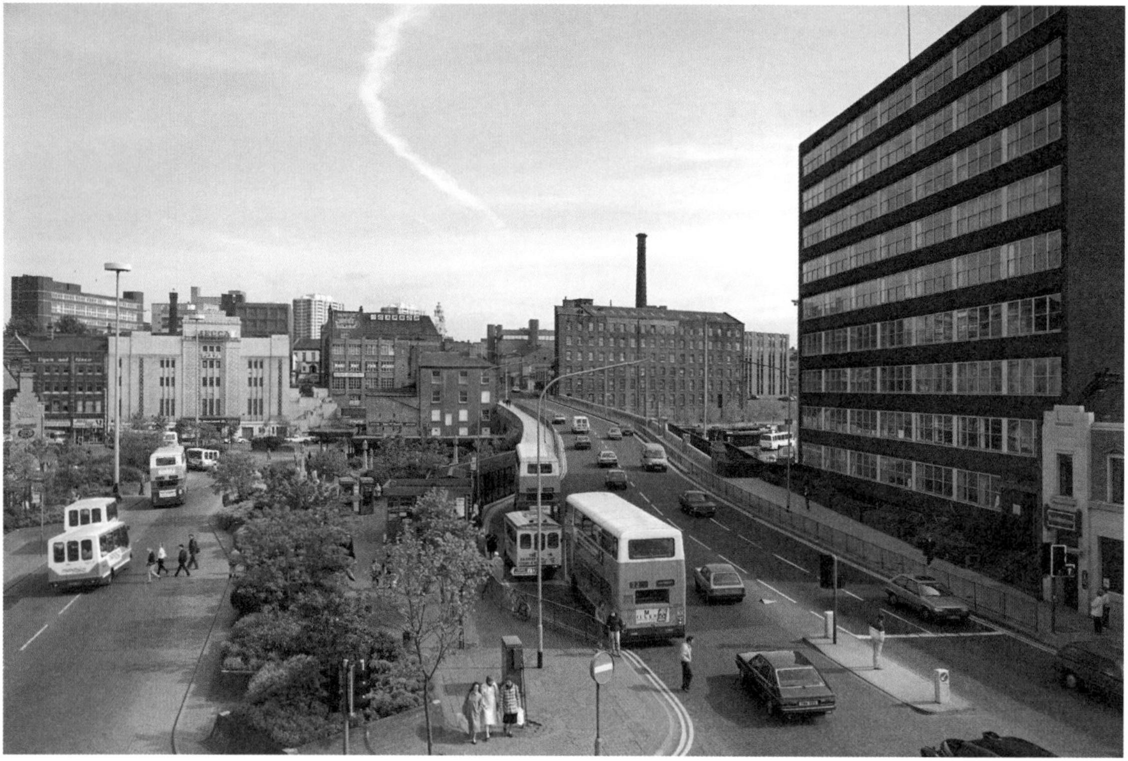

The photographs of John Davies are family trees too, with buildings instead of people indicating change. These epic views of towns owe much to Davies' interest in how cities work, showing how we live with the Industrial Revolution every day.

This broadside, written in 1873, imagines a world 100 years hence; it is a sci-fi nursery rhyme of nonsense and freedom, including sexual emancipation. The line about 'Brigham Young' refers to the Mormon leader. American Mormons escaped persecution in their homeland and cannily settled in the expanding industrial centres of the UK, where new religions could offer some form of order amongst the confusion of the city life. The photograph of Adrian Street and his father was taken in 1973 (page 28), and perhaps he even exceeded the broadside writer's expectations of life in the future. The reality was a little more mundane – the images on the following pages are stills from Super-8 home movies all filmed in 1973.

Fig. 58
John Davies
Mersey Square, Stockport
1986

Fig. 59
'A Prophecy for 1973'
1873

A PROPHECY FOR 1973.

Written by Thomas Yates, *of Blackburn.*

Tune:—"The Henpecked Club."

(*Copyright.*)

NOW they tell us this world's ne'er at an end,
But to prove its contray, is what I intend,
In a song what I've wrote, if you live you will see
In One thousand Nine hundred and Seventy three,
I was dreaming last night, and I prophesied plain,
That the world has turned over and over again,
And everything changed, that I plainly could see,
In One thousand Nine hundred and Seventy three.

Chorus:

Oh, Dear! Oh, dear! what things you will see,
In One thousand Nine hundred and Seventy three

No governmet laws we shall have, it is true,
There will be no Magistrates, no Bobbys in blue
To charge "*Ten Bob and Costs*," when a man's
been on the spree, [lives,
You can drink like a fish, far down in the sea:
You can act *Brigham Young*, all the days of your
And if *one's not enough*, you can get forty wives,
If you are tired of *one*, or she turns out *a bore*,
Get another and *send her* to the chap next door.

Everyone will be rich, there will be no need to beg
Nor stump up and down, with an old wooden leg
If your limbs are blown off, with a bullet or breeze
The Doctors will replace you new one's with ease
And children, then they will hatch them by steam
And feed them with nutmegs, blacklead or cream
And they will grow to such a size, you can tell,
They can peep o'er the moon, and look down
into *H—l.*

Young lovers, you'll see them in dozs. and crowds
Courting by moonlight, on the top of the clouds,
And if a wet evening, around them should creep,
They can drop through the skylight *to bed* and
And pigs will commence flying up in the air,[asleep
And men flying after them everywhere,
So then, if Pork stakes you should want for to fry
Live pigs will drop down ready cook'd from the sky

Then Bullocks you'll see, wearing ladies kid gloves
And Billy-goats turned into young Turtle Doves,
And Jack-asses, walking about all the day,
In Parsons' black gowns, with the Shakers to pray
And Elephants, working the Sewing Machine.
And making wheel-barrows to travel by steam,
Red Herrings will starch Paper collars and Cuffs
And Mangles *be turned* into young ladies Muffs.

760.

DOWN BY THE VILLAGE WELL.

Ladies' Version, (Copyright.)

By L. M. Thornton.

'TWAS in the spring not long ago,
I lived in Lincolnshire;
And often to the well did go,
For water sweet and clear.
One morning I the handle turned,
To let the bucket down,
When such a fine young man I saw,
Dressed in a suit of Brown.

Chorus.

Down by the village well,
Down by the village well,
'Twas there that Harry charm'd me quite,
Down by the village well.

A twelvemonth from that very time,
He came a courting me;
And no one more affectionate,
I'm sure than him could be.
With joy I leant upon his arm,
As far we used to stray,
And sighed when at the hour of ten,
Adieu I had to say.

The ring is on, the bells have rung,
A little cot I share,
And whosoever enters it,
Will find that peace is there.
It was a lucky day for me,
(I'm proud the truth to tell,)
When charming Harry I beheld,
Down by the villiage well.

:oXo:

Boot-jacks will be *turned* into Gooseberry Pies,
And Cod-fish will be turned into Crickets & Fies
All other Fishes will turn into Beef in each brook
You can draw out a 40lb. lump, with a hook;
And Bobbies will turn into Lobsters and Crabs,
And Churches be turned into Coaches and Cabs,
Then Bishops and Parsons will turn it is clear,
To sweep Chimneys and live on the soot all the
year.

There will be no Old People, they'll always be
young, [tongue,
Men will not be plagued with a cross woman's
Bum-bailiffs will swallow the County Court then,
Old Nick will be loose, upon earth once again;
The Sun and the Moon, will be changed never fear
Into large Suet Dumplings, and Barrels of Beer,
Teetotallers will turn into Water Butts free,
If you doubt it, just go to *Old Davy* and see.

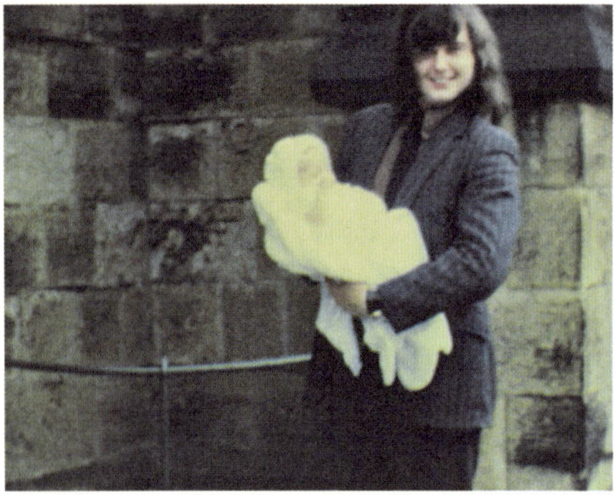

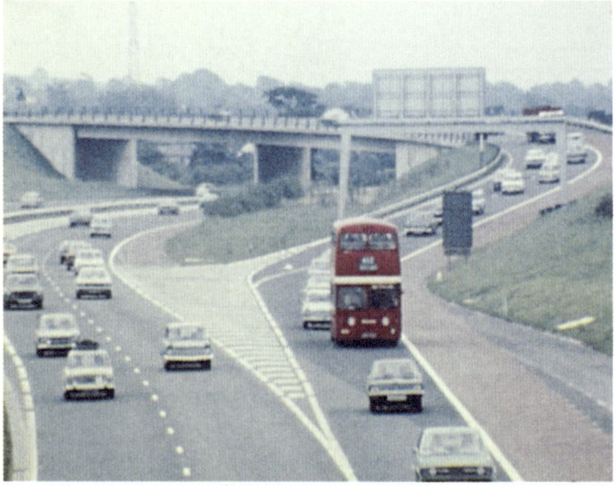

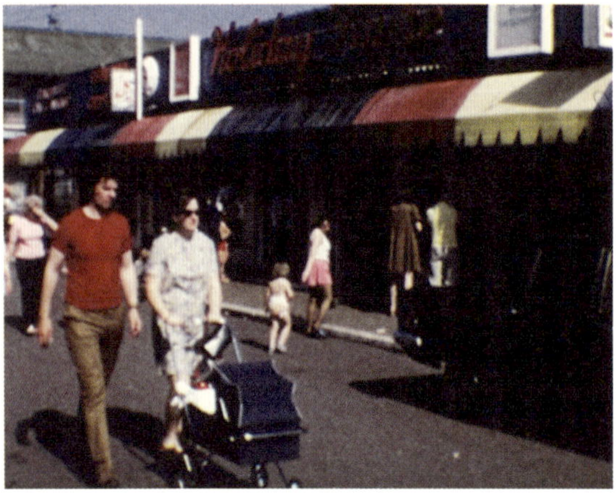

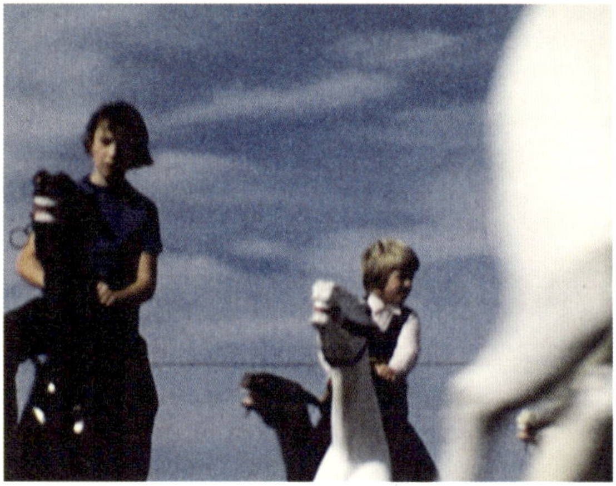

Fig. 60
(top left)
Rachael's Christening
1973

Fig. 61
(top right)
Traffic in Central Lancashire
1973

Fig. 62
(bottom)
7 Days in Butlinland
1973

Fig. 63
7 Days in Butlinland
1973

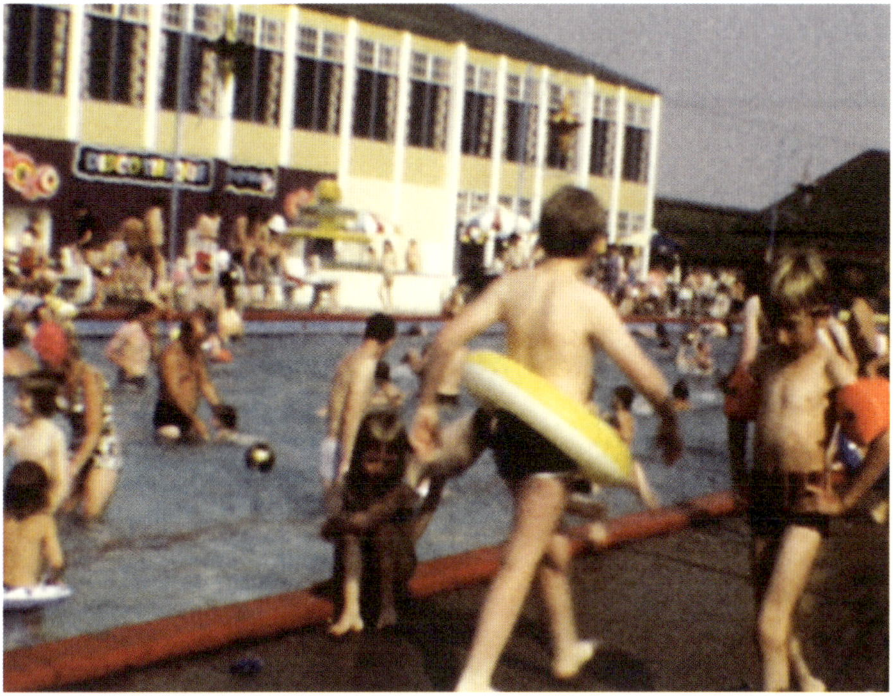

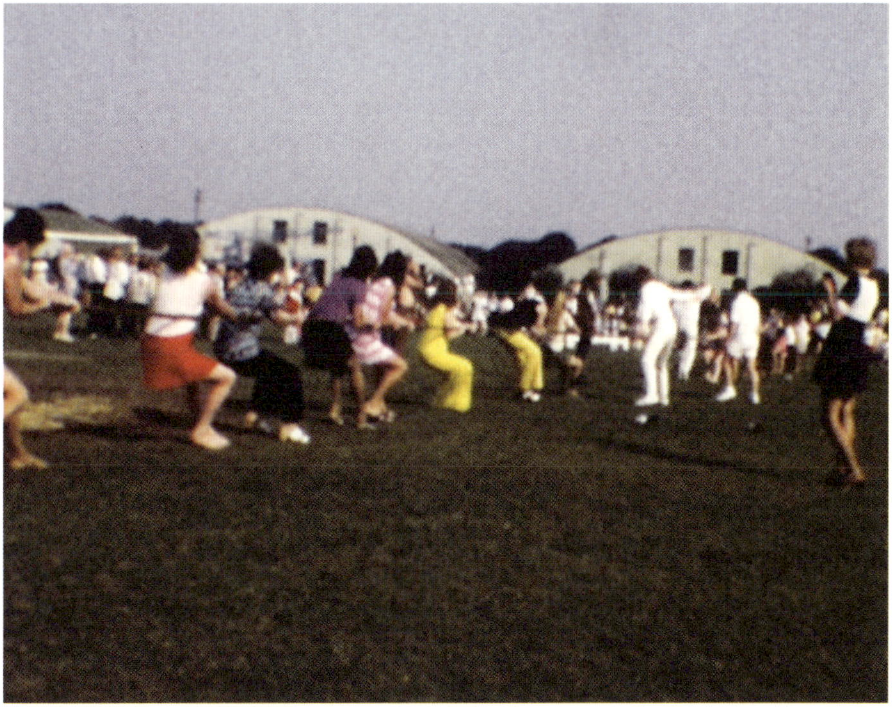

Afterword and Thanks

Roger Malbert
Senior Curator, Hayward Touring

All that Is Solid Melts into Air is a quotation from Marx and Engels.[1] It was translated from the original German into English via Prospero's speech in *The Tempest*, which ends, 'We are such stuff/As dreams are made on; and our little life/Is rounded with a sleep' – a distinctly anti-materialist thought. *All that Is Solid Melts into Air* was also the title of an influential work of Marxist sociology in the 1980s by Marshall Berman, subtitled *The Experience of Modernity*. This trail of references is worth mentioning in the context of a project concerned with lineage. The society we have inherited, the towns and cities of England, the social formations, cultural traditions, class divisions, inequalities of wealth and opportunity, derive to an overwhelming extent from the nineteenth century, the age of the Industrial Revolution and the British Empire. If, to quote Marx again, 'the tradition of all the dead generations weighs like a nightmare on the brain of the living',[2] there may be more reasons for reflecting on this period in English history than we might immediately realise.

As an artist who rejoices in people, as both the subject and often the medium of his work, Jeremy Deller is naturally less interested in utilitarian assessments of the economic benefits of the Industrial Revolution than in imagining the lived experience of the young men and women, adolescents and children, who toiled in the factories and mines that produced Britain's wealth. Deller's breadth of sympathies and his engagement with popular culture, especially music, give a particular emphasis to his perspective on this history. Deller has been described by Hayward Gallery Director, Ralph Rugoff, as 'a social cartographer revealing neglected ley lines of cultural history'; here he is also a social archaeologist, uncovering affinities and connections across historical epochs and finding new meanings in familiar images and stories. The dead are – in our imaginations – coexistent with the living. Their songs, complaints and protests, represented here in quotations, broadsides and song-sheets, resonate with those of our own time.

All that Is Solid Melts into Air has been curated by Jeremy Deller for Hayward Touring. We are indebted to him for his extraordinary generosity and commitment to both the book and the exhibition, which exemplify his highly personal, free-ranging and egalitarian approach to art and politics. The idea for the exhibition was first explored in a project at Palais de Tokyo, Paris in 2008. Many of the images of the Industrial Revolution here – prints, photographs and drawings – have rarely been seen, others may be familiar as documents of social history, while a certain number are accredited works of high art. Deller's lateral interpretation of this diverse material offers a fresh context in which hierarchies are dissolved; printed ephemera and historical artefacts and texts are shown alongside and on equal terms with major paintings; and analogies are drawn between the (brutal) past and the (indifferent) present. Importantly, the exhibition, although containing a wealth of historical material, is in essence a contemporary project – and a work of art in its own right.

Artist-curators James N. Hutchinson and Lesley Young have provided essential curatorial and logistical support, initiating and researching many aspects of the exhibition. Jeremy Deller's artistic collaborators, banner-maker Ed Hall and muralist Stuart Sam Hughes, are producing new works for the show, and a selection of industrial sounds and music has been assembled for a jukebox. The folk music historian Roy Palmer has given us invaluable guidance and Scott King lent his expertise to the design of the Shaun Ryder family tree.

We would like to thank all of our lenders, both institutions and individuals: Anson Engine Museum; Blackburn Museum and Art Gallery and the Sharples Family; Bradford Museum and Galleries; British Film Institute; Chetham's Library, Manchester; John Davies; Harris Museum and Art Gallery, Preston; Laing Art Gallery, Newcastle; Manchester Art Gallery; Manchester Libraries, Information and Archives; Museum of Science and Industry, Manchester; National Museum of Wales; Motorola Solutions; North West Film Archive at Manchester Metropolitan University; North West Sound Archives, Clitheroe; People's History Museum, Manchester; Ben Roberts; Science Museum; Adrian Street; Peter Kennedy Collection at the British Library Sound Archive; and Gavin Watson.

Many individuals have shared their knowledge and enthusiasm, and without them the exhibition would not have been possible: Keith Badder, Jukebox Selection Co.; Sue Bannister, genealogist; Kevin Bolton, Manchester Libraries, Information and Archives; Duncan Broady, Greater Manchester Police Museum; Sallyann Browning, Museum of Science and Industry (MoSI); Geoff Challinor, MBE; Anson Engine Museum; Neil Child-Dyer, The Work Foundation; Andrew Davies, University of Liverpool; Tony Dykes, British Film Institute; Phil Dunn, People's History Museum, Manchester; Mark Etheridge, National Museum Wales (NMW); Oliver Fairclough, NMW; Mark Furness, John Rylands Library, University of Manchester (JRL); Clare Grundy, Manchester Art Gallery; Stella Halkyard, JRL; David Hendy; Emma Heslewood, Harris Museum, Preston; Marion Hewitt, North West Film Archive (NWFA); Rebecca Hill, Blackburn Museum and Art Gallery; Gail Hunter, Paisley Museum; Boris Jardine, Science Museum; Susan Jeffrey, Paisley Museum; Kevin Johnson, Science Museum; Jack Kirby, MoSI; Meg McHugh, MoSI; Beth McIntyre, NMW; Will McTaggart, NWFA; Roy Palmer; Maggie Pedley, Bradford Museums and Galleries; Michael Powell, Chetham's Library, Manchester; all at Quarry Bank Mill, National Trust; Nic Rayner, Greater Manchester County Record Office; Jennifer Reid, researcher and performer; Steve Roud, author; Andrew Schofield, North West Sound Archive, Clitheroe; Janet Small, Black Country Living Museum; Philippa Smith, London Metropolitan Archives; Laura Smyth, The Vaughan Williams Memorial Library, English Folk Dance and Song Society (EFDSS); Malcolm Taylor, EFDSS; Dr. Matt Thompson, Ironbridge Gorge Museum; Nicholas Thornton, NMW; Vanessa Toulmin, National Fairground Archive, The University of Sheffield (NFA);

I. M. Trowell, NFA; Shane and Aaron at Vinyl Carvers, London; Sandra Underwood, Ances-Tree Family History Research; Pauline Webb, MoSI; Kathy Whalen, Chetham's Library, Manchester; Katherine White, Trowbridge Museum; Emily Yates, Science Museum.

Thanks to colleagues at our partner galleries on the tour: Manchester Art Gallery, Maria Balshaw, Director, and Tim Wilcox, Curator; Nottingham Castle Museum & Art Gallery, Deborah Dean, Visual Arts and Collections Manager, and Tristram Aver, Exhibitions Officer; Mead Gallery, University of Warwick, Sarah Shalgosky, Curator, and Fiona Venables, Assistant Curator; Laing Art Gallery, Newcastle, Julie Milne, Chief of Art Galleries and Lesley Richardson, Assistant Keeper.

Hayward Touring Assistant Curators Vanessa North and – following Vanessa's departure – Gillian Fox have organised the exhibition with unparalleled dedication, energy and resourcefulness. This publication has been produced by Hayward Art Publisher, Ben Fergusson, and Editor, Faye Robson, and we owe them immense thanks for their skilful editing, patience and flexibility, whilst Hettie Judah has provided crucial support in the creation of the text in this book. The graphic designers, A Practice for Everyday Life, have been instrumental in helping us to conceptualise both the book and the exhibition and their contribution to the project cannot be overstated.

At Southbank Centre we thank Ralph Rugoff, Director, Hayward Gallery, Alan Bishop, Chief Executive, Jude Kelly, Artistic Director, and Sarah O'Reilly, General Manager, Hayward Gallery, for their ongoing support, and the following colleagues in the Hayward Gallery and Touring team for their essential contributions: Dave Bell, Steve Bullas, Mark King and Dave Palmer, Senior Technicians; Peter Brown and Ben Hudson, Transport Technicians; Ruth Pelopida, Hayward Operations Manager; Marcia Ceppo, Hayward Operations Coordinator; Vicky Skelding-Bloor, Registrar; Alison Maun, Bookings and Transport Administrator; Oliver Krug, Visual Arts Press Manager; Nadine Monem, Hayward Publisher; Steve Burridge and Sarah Cashman, Picture Researchers.

[1] The full quotation reads: 'All that is solid melts into air, all that is holy is profaned, and man is at last compelled to face with sober senses his real conditions of life, and his relations with his kind.' Karl Marx/Friedrich Engels, *The Communist Manifesto*, 1848
[2] Karl Marx, *The Eighteenth Brumaire of Louis Napoleon*, 1852

List of Works

All measurements are given in centimetres, height x width x depth. Numbers by works denote plates in catalogue.

List of Exhibited Works

Anonymous/Unknown

Employ Only Best British Workmen, date unknown
Enamel on metal
40 x 79
Bradford Museums & Galleries

64 *We Are the Lions of the Industry*, c. 1910
Enamel on metal
46 x 114
Bradford Museums & Galleries

James Sharples as a Smith, date unknown
Albumen print photograph
45.5 x 31.5
People's History Museum, Manchester

14 *Photograph of James Sharples (Oval Cameo)*, date unknown
Carte de visite albumen print photograph
16.5 x 10.7
People's History Museum, Manchester

A Kiln for Burning Coke, near Maidstone, Kent, 1799
Aquatint print, with hand colouring
54 x 45.5
Science Museum, London

Effects of Alston Brewery, c. 1805
Pencil drawing with red ink
20 x 26
Science Museum, London

23 *Miner with Candle, Climbing Ladder*, c. 1805
Pen and sepia wash on paper
23 x 19
Science Museum, London

30 *Double-dial Longcase Clock from Park Green Silk Mill, Macclesfield*, c. 1810
Wood and metal
147 x 62 x 28
Museum of Science and Industry, Manchester

Pully System to Connect Double-dial Longcase Clock to Park Green Silk Mill, Macclesfield, c. 1810
Wood, rope and metal
Dimensions variable
Museum of Science and Industry, Manchester

Smoke Consuming at Ancoats, Manchester, 1820
Etching
38 x 27
Science Museum, London

'Owdham Town at Dinnertime', early nineteenth century
Black-and-white printed, single-sheet letterpress
10 x 25.3
Manchester Libraries, Information and Archives, Manchester City Council

'Salford Bastille', early nineteenth century
Printed black-and-white, single-sheet letterpress
17 x 21.1
Manchester Libraries, Information and Archives, Manchester City Council

40 'The New Bury Loom',
early nineteenth century
From a book of
collected broadsides
6.6 x 23.2, in book 37 x 26 x 3.5
Manchester Libraries,
Information and Archives,
Manchester City Council

41 'Utick's Trip to Manchester',
early nineteenth century
Printed black-and-white,
single-sheet letterpress
18.3 x 24.8
Manchester Libraries,
Information and Archives,
Manchester City Council

32 *Rules to Be Observed in this Factory from Thomas Ainsworth & Sons., Church Street Mills, Preston*, c. 1830
55.7 x 44.2
Printed poster on paper
(printed by Pritt, Preston)
Harris Museum & Art Gallery,
Preston

Towers Yard Factory Bell, 1835
Metal, rope
Cast by Thomas Mears of London
in the Whitechapel Bell Foundry
Dimensions variable
Anson Engine Museum, Poynton

'Things that Ought Not to Be',
from a book of Manchester
songs and ballads compiled by
Robert Holt, c. 1843–73
Album comprising 424 broadsides
6 x 24 x 31
Chetham's Library, Manchester

'Victoria Bridge on a Saturday
Night', from a book of Manchester
songs and ballads compiled by
Robert Holt, c. 1843–73
Album comprising 424 broadsides
6 x 24 x 31
Chetham's Library, Manchester

59 'A Prophecy for 1973', c. 1860
Printed black-and-white,
single-sheet letterpress
19.5 x 25
Chetham's Library, Manchester

'Five in the Morning', c. 1860
Printed black-and-white,
single-sheet letterpress
19.5 x 25
Chetham's Library, Manchester

42 'Jone O' Grinfield', c. 1860
Printed black-and-white,
single-sheet letterpress
19.5 x 25
Chetham's Library, Manchester

'Just What We'd All Like to See',
c. 1860
Printed black-and-white,
single-sheet letterpress
19.5 x 25
Chetham's Library, Manchester

'Lines upon the Explosion
at Witton', c. 1860
Printed black-and-white,
single-sheet letterpress
19.5 x 25
Chetham's Library, Manchester

Shaft Cage of the Hester Pit, New Hartley, Showing its Construction and Damage Following the Breakage of the Beam in January, 1862
Lithographic print
21.6 x 27.9
Discovery Museum, Newcastle
upon Tyne

34 *Amalgamated Engineers' Union Banner*, 1890
Painted cotton sateen
237 x 237
Laing Art Gallery, Newcastle
upon Tyne

17 *Steel*, 1945
Colour film; dir.: Ronald Riley; cinematographer: Jack Cardiff
35 minutes
British Film Institute

36 *Motorola WT4000 Wearable Terminal*, 2013
Plastic and electronics
2.6 x 9.3 x 14.2
Courtesy Motorola Solutions

Thomas Allom
Swainson Birley Cotton Mill near Preston, Lancashire, 1834
Pencil drawing with pen, sepia and wash
12 x 19
Science Museum, London

J. Bluck (after R. H. Marten)
13 *Salt Mine, Cheshire*, 1814
Coloured aquatint engraving
15 x 25
Science Museum, London

G. F. Bragg
10 *Treforest Tin Works, Glamorganshire*, c.1840
Hand-coloured lithograph
50.8 x 68.5
National Museum Wales, Cardiff

A. R. Burt
38 *John Evans*, 1819
Engraving with wash on paper
28.6 x 20.6
National Museum Wales, Cardiff

W. J. Chapman
47 Selection from *Francis Crawshay Workers Portraits*, 1835
16 paintings, oil on linen
Each 36.3 x 25.6
National Museum Wales, Cardiff

George Childs
Dowlais Ironworks, c. 1840
Watercolour over pencil on paper
23.8 x 34.8
National Museum Wales, Cardiff

William Clayton
1–5 *Iron Workers, Tredegar, Wales*, 1865
28 cartes de visite albumen photographic prints
Dimensions variable
Manchester City Galleries

John Davies
58 *Mersey Square, Stockport*, 1986
Silver gelatin photograph
71.3 x 104
Courtesy of Michael Hoppen Contemporary

57 *Stockport Viaduct*, 1986
Silver gelatin photograph
71.3 x 104
Courtesy of Michael Hoppen Contemporary

Jeremy Deller
Hallelujah! Shaun Ryder's Family Tree, 2008
Vinyl lettering on wall
Dimensions variable
Courtesy the artist
Design: Scott King

28 *So Many Ways to Hurt You (The Life and Times of Adrian Street)*, 2010
Digitised film as part of mixed-media installation, with wrestling costumes
Dimensions variable
Courtesy the artist

There's a New Sensation: Bryan Ferry's Family Tree, 2013
Vinyl lettering on wall
Dimensions variable
Courtesy the artist

Jukebox, 2013
Jukebox with sound and music recordings, with mural backdrop by Stuart Sam Hughes
Dimensions variable
Courtesy the artist

Audio Recording of the Weaving Shed at Queen Street Mill at High Volume, 2013
Sound piece
Continuous on a loop
Courtesy the artist and North West Sound Archive

60–63 *Promotional Film for All that Is Solid Melts into Air*, 2013
Projected video
Approx 16 mins
Courtesy the artist

Take Me Back Home: Noddy Holder's Family Tree, 2013
Vinyl lettering on wall
Dimensions variable
Courtesy the artist

Hello, Today you have day off, 2013
Fabric banner made by Ed Hall
Dimensions variable
Courtesy the artist

35 *Zero-Hour Contract*, 2013
Printed paper
Dimensions variable
Courtesy the artist

G. Greatbach (after H. Warren)
9 *'The Black Country' near Bilston*, 1869
Engraving
23 x 29
Science Museum, London

Robert Havell (after George Walker)
Factory Children, 1814
Hand-coloured aquatint
26 x 36
Science Museum, London

The Collier, 1814
Hand-coloured aquatint
25.5 x 34.5
Science Museum, London

Thomas Hornor
18 *Rolling Mills, Merthyr Tydfil*, 1819
Watercolour on paper
41.4 x 54.2
National Museum Wales, Cardiff

Attributed to G. Jameson
A Keelman Getting his Orders, c. 1811
Watercolour on paper
16.4 x 12.8
Laing Art Gallery, Newcastle

21 *A Pitman Going to Work*, c. 1811
Watercolour on paper
16.2 x 12.9
Laing Art Gallery, Newcastle

Judas Priest
19 *Unleashed in the East*, 1979
12-inch album in sleeve
Private collection

Dennis Hutchinson
26 *Adrian Street with his Father at the Pithead of Brynmawr Colliery, Wales*, 1973
Black-and-white photographic reproduction
Dimensions variable
Courtesy Jeremy Deller

S. Lacey (after H. Gastineau)
Nant y Glo, Monmouthshire, c. 1835
Engraving
12.3 x 17.9
Science Museum, London

J. W. Lowry (after James Nasmyth)
31 *Thomas Robinson's Power Loom Factory, Stockport*, 1849–50
Engraving
17.5 x 32
Science Museum, London

John Martin
6–8 *The Destruction of Sodom and Gomorrah*, 1852
Oil on canvas
136.3 x 212.3
Laing Art Gallery, Newcastle upon Tyne

Newman & Co.

12 *Penrhyn Slate Quarries, near Bangor, Wales*, 1842
Lithograph
28 x 39
Science Museum, London

William Pickett

'Iron Works, Colebrook Dale', from *The Romantic and Picturesque Scenery of England and Wales*, 1805
Hand-coloured aquatint engraving
45 x 33
Science Museum, London

Ben Roberts

65 *Adam Hoccom, Facilities and Engineering, Amazon Fulfilment Centre, Rugeley*, 2013
C-type photographic print
190 x 127
Courtesy the artist

37 *Amazon Fulfilment Centre, Towers Business Park, Rugeley*, 2013
C-type photographic print
190 x 127
Courtesy the artist

Bev Horton, Outbound Despatch, Amazon Fulfilment Centre, Rugeley, 2013
C-type photographic print
190 x 127
Courtesy the artist

James Sharples

Sheet of Anatomical Details, Blackburn School of Art, Aged 18 (Muscle Study), 1843
Lithograph
53.4 x 74.5
People's History Museum, Manchester

15 *Sketch of Forearm (detail from The Forge)*, date unknown
Pencil on paper
14.3 x 18.5
People's History Museum, Manchester

The Forge, c. 1848
Oil on canvas
129 x 169
Blackburn Museum and Art Gallery and the Sharples family

16 *The Smithy*, (published by the executive estate of the late James Sharples), 1894
Goupil gravure
43 x 62
People's History Museum, Manchester

Dean Shaw

39 *Tony Iommi, Black Sabbath, Donnington*, 2012
Digital C-type photographic print
42 x 29.7
Courtesy the artist

Adrian Street

Union Jack Cape, 1969
Majestic metallic lamé, reversible
Length: 150
Courtesy Adrian Street

Purple Gown, 1971
Yellow satin brocade and velvet, decorated with lace and rhinestones
Length: 150
Courtesy Adrian Street

Ian Tilton

55 *Happy Mondays – Bridge*, 1987
Black-and-white photographic print
42 x 29.7
Courtesy the artist

53 *Happy Mondays – Cinema*, 1987
Black-and-white photographic print
42 x 29.7
Courtesy the artist

Happy Mondays – Marina, 1987
Black-and-white photographic print
42 x 29.7
Courtesy the artist

54 *Happy Mondays – Mural*, 1987
Black-and-white
photographic print
42 x 29.7
Courtesy the artist

Gavin Watson
11 *Slough Centre, End of the Night*, 1989
42 x 29.7
Courtesy the artist

Images in Publication Only

Anonymous / Unknown

46 *Merthyr Rising*, 1831
Etching

22 *Girl with Belt and Chain Dragging Coal Tubs Underground*
Published in *Parliamentary Papers*, 1842
Etching

33 *Preston Lock-Out*, 1853
Ink and watercolour on paper
Lancashire Archives

48–52 *Police Book Containing Images of 'Scuttlers'*, c. 1884
Record book and photographs
Greater Manchester Police Museum

25 *Adrian Street as Teddy Boy* (second from right), *Wales*, c. 1957
Black-and-white photograph
Courtesy Adrian Street Archive

24 *Adrian Street Bodybuilding*, 1975
C-type photograph
Courtesy Adrian Street Archive

27 *Adrian Street at an Airport in the US with his Valet, Miss Linda*, Mid-1980s
C-type photograph
Courtesy Adrian Street Archive

John Martin
8 *Plan for Preventing the Pollution of the Water of the Thames*, 1834
Etching
City of London, London Metropolitan Archives

REX / Andre Csillag
20 *Judas Priest – K K Downing, Dave Holland, Rob Halford, Ian Hill and Glenn Tipton, London*, 1981
Black-and-white photograph

Copyright credits

Photographic credits

All images are courtesy the lender, unless otherwise stated. Courtesy the artist 56; Adrian Street Archive 24, 25, 26, 27, 28; Anson Engine Museum, Poynton 29; Greater Manchester Police Museum and Archives (Matthew Bend) 48, 49, 50, 51, 52; © Laing Art Gallery, Newcastle upon Tyne (Tyne & Wear Archives & Museums) 6, 7, 21, 34; 'Mr. Large Firm', Preston Lockout Cartoons, Lancashire Archives (DDPR 138/87a) 33; © Manchester Art Gallery 1, 3, 4, 5; © National Museum of Wales 10, 18, 38, 44, 47; by permission of People's History Museum 14, 15, 16; REX / Andre Csillag 20; © Science Museum / Science & Society Picture Library. All rights reserved. 9, 12, 13, 23, 31, 43, 45.

Published on the occasion of the exhibition
Jeremy Deller: All that Is Solid Melts into Air

Manchester Art Gallery
11 October 2013 – 19 January 2014

Nottingham Castle Museum
and Art Gallery
31 January – 22 April 2014

Mead Gallery
University of Warwick, Coventry
3 May – 21 June 2014

Laing Art Gallery, Newcastle
12 July – 26 October 2014

Exhibition curated by Jeremy Deller, with James Hutchinson and Lesley Young. Exhibition organised by Vanessa North and Gillian Fox.

This exhibition has been made possible by the provision of insurance through the Government Indemnity Scheme. Hayward Touring, London, would like to thank HM Government for providing Government Indemnity and the Department for Culture, Media and Sport and Arts Council England for arranging the indemnity.

Published by Hayward Publishing
Southbank Centre, Belvedere Road
London, SE1 8XX, UK
www.southbankcentre.co.uk

Art Publisher: Ben Fergusson / Nadine Monem
Staff Editor: Faye Robson
Sales Officer: Alex Glen
Press & Marketing Coordinator: Diana Adell
Catalogue Design: A Practice for Everyday Life
Colour Management: Dexter Pre-Media
Printing: Henry Ling, Dorset

A catalogue record for this book is available from the British Library.

ISBN 978 1 85332 319 5

Distributed in North America, Central America and South America by
D.A.P. / Distributed Art Publishers, Inc.,
155 Sixth Avenue, 2nd Floor, New York, NY 10013
Tel. +212 627 1999
Fax. +212 627 9484
www.artbook.com

Distributed in the UK and Europe by Cornerhouse Publications
70 Oxford Street, Manchester, M1 5NH
Tel. +44 (0)161 200 1503
Fax. +44 (0)161 200 1504
www.cornerhouse.org/books

HAYWARD TOURING
SOUTHBANK CENTRE

LOTTERY FUNDED
Supported using public funding by
ARTS COUNCIL ENGLAND